1000+ STILL USEFUL

and how to use them in your writing

An Experimental Play on Words

with Laura Grebe and Reji Laberje

Quantity order requests can be emailed to:
publishing@rejilaberje.com

Or mailed to:
Reji Laberje Writing and Publishing
Publishing Orders
234 W. Broadway Street
Waukesha, WI 53186

Grebe, Laura
1000+ Still Useful Words
Contributing Author: Reji Laberje
Contributing Editor: Reji Laberje
Cover Design: Michael Nicloy
Interior Layout: Reji Laberje

ISBN: 1945907088
ISBN-13: 978-1945907081

SALES Categories:
Reference / Writing, Research & Publishing Guides / Writing
Humor & Entertainment / Humor / Puns & Wordplay
Reference / Dictionaries & Thesauruses / Synonyms & Antonyms

BISAC Codes:
LAN021000Language Arts & Disciplines / Vocabulary
LAN005000Language Arts & Disciplines / Composition & Creative Writing
HUM019000Humor / Topic / Language

Writing and Publishing
www.rejilaberje.com

For God, love, the Doctor, iced tea, all those who have lost words and been unable to find them, and Nancy Drew.

~Laura

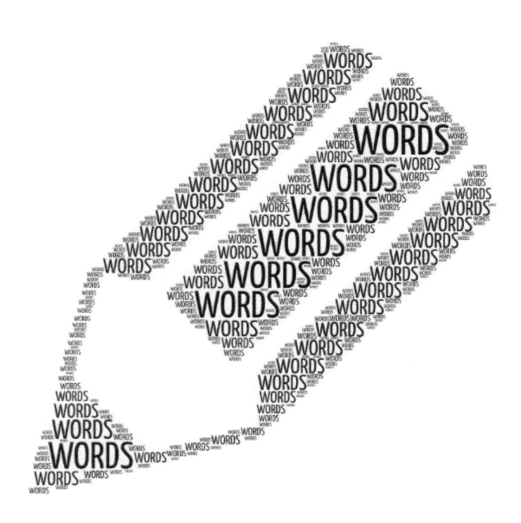

Foreword

Have you ever struggled to find just the right word, but you don't seem to have anything suitable in your....mind? No. Suitable in your . . . notebook . . . collection . . . ensemble? No. Anthology? That's not it either! Something more like skill set . . . skillset . . . two accepted spellings . . . ugh!

Have you ever struggled to find just the right word, but you don't seem to have anything suitable on the tip-of-your-tongue . . . on your lips . . . in your back pocket? Front pocket? Frontal lobe?

Scratch that. Have you ever struggled to find just the right word, but end up resorting to SHIFT + F7 and then just pick any word because you've had it up to here . . . up to your neck . . . up to your eyebrows? Or you can't waste anymore time so you just go with whatever it was you thought of last?

Don't settle for the words Microsoft (or,<insert other file- . . . document- . . . word- creation software here>) hand-picked for you . . . auto-generated for you.

You deserve more than that!

What follows is a list of 1000+ (give-or-take . . . mostly give) words that may be sitting just off the beaten path but are still useful in writing today. These are words that everybody should have on-hand. Keep them close. Use them to spark ideas.

Even if the right word for you didn't make the list, use the list as inspiration . . . encouragement to FIND . . . locate . . . discover . . . decide upon your perfect word.

Then you won't have to struggle to find the perfect word . . . phrase . . . utterance . . . bleep (not here—well, maybe implied!) . . . blurt . . . language . . . because you'll have all these letters that form meanings at-the-ready, in your. . . in your . . . in your . . . (we've come full-circle . . . back around) . . . at-the-ready, in your
REPERTOIRE!

Dagnab it!

~Laura

About this Book and Publisher

Laura works with Reji Laberje Writing and Publishing for her Experimental Word Play books and other publications.

We have an awesome online place with cool stuff . . . video, audio, downloadables and social media mayhem. You can learn about Laura, her books, really wicked awesome stuff like these lists, and so much more . . . yadda, yadda, yadda . . . etc. . . . and the like. We call it her "Electronic Resource Hub", or, ERH.

I personally can't wait to see what happens. Laura's like our own personal grammar girl . . . but with word banks – Word Girl!

In fact, if you check back, and back, and back, we'll be adding, and adding, and adding to it. You'll find—not just really cool Experimental Word Play stuff, but also her upcoming "Cupcake Therapy" book, a maternity journal like no other, and eventually books ranging from children's mysteries to Patent Law?

Yeah. We know. She's pretty flipping impressive. We love her, too!

At any rate, you can visit Laura Grebe's ERH by scanning the code below or, for the "old-fashioned" non-smart device users, we even put the interweb address below the code. Feel free to type that puppy in on your laptop . . . desktop . . . tower . . . Apple 2GE . . . to get to all those cool ERH goodies and also check out a bunch of other useful knowledge on her publisher's site.

When you do give in to the digital peer pressure, we say "Thanks" . . . "Merci" . . . "Gracias" . . . and, of course, "Danke" for dropping by!

Yours in writing,
Reji Laberje and Laura's Publishing Team!

Laura Grebe – Electronic Resource Hub
www.rejilaberje.com/laura-grebe.html

A Still Useful Table of Contents

Be mindful when it comes to your words. A string of some that don't mean much to you, may stick with someone else for a lifetime.
                                        ~Rachel Wolchin

1

"The Still Useful Words List"

No categories or explanations, yet. Those will all come. Here, simply, is the list of the 1000 or so words that will eventually fall into categories including:

- Foods
- Beverages
- Random Objects
- Colors
- Weather
- Clothing
- Earth (the planet and her topography)
- Animals
- City (architecture and urban settings)
- Home (a household and the people in it)

Oh! And you'll also learn how those different categories can uniquely affect your writing!

1.	2-LITER SODA	45.	BARREN
2.	ABSINTH	46.	BARRETTE
3.	ACORN	47.	BASEBALL
4.	ACQUIDUCT	48.	BASEBALL CAP
5.	ADVIL ®	49.	BASEMENT
6.	AIR	50.	BASKET
7.	AIRPLANE	51.	BATHROOM
8.	ALARM CLOCK	52.	BATHTUB
9.	ALE	53.	BEAUTIFUL
10.	ALGAE	54.	BEAVER
11.	ALLEY	55.	BED
12.	ALLIGATOR	56.	BEDDING
13.	AMARETTO	57.	BEDROOM
14.	AMOEBA	58.	BEE
15.	ANKLET	59.	BEEF
16.	ANT	60.	BEER
17.	ANTHILL	61.	BEETLE
18.	APPLE	62.	BEIGE
19.	APPLE CIDER	63.	BELT
20.	APPLE JUICE	64.	BIKE SHORTS
21.	APPLETINI	65.	BIKES
22.	APRON	66.	BIKINI
23.	APTHONG	67.	BIRD
24.	AQUAMARINE	68.	BIRD BATH
25.	ARCADE	69.	BISQUE
26.	ARCHIPELAGO	70.	BITE-SIZED CANDY BAR
27.	ARCHWAY	71.	BLACK
28.	ARID	72.	BLACK TEA
29.	ART	73.	BLACKTOP
30.	ART DECO	74.	BLANKET
31.	ART DISTRICT	75.	BLEAK
32.	ARTICHOKE	76.	BLINDING
33.	AUBERGINE	77.	BLISTERING
34.	AUBURN	78.	BLOOD
35.	AVENUE	79.	BLOOMERS
36.	AVOCADO	80.	BLOSSOM
37.	BABY DOLL	81.	BLOUSE
38.	BACON BIT	82.	BLUE
39.	BAHAMA MAMA	83.	BLUEBERRY
40.	BALLOON	84.	BLUSH WINE
41.	BALMY	85.	BLUSTERY
42.	BANANA SPLIT	86.	BOARD GAMES
43.	BANDEAU	87.	BOBBER
44.	BAR	88.	BONNET

89.	BOOKS	133.	CADET
90.	BOOKSHELF	134.	CAKE
91.	BOOTS	135.	CALM
92.	BOULDER	136.	CAMISOLE
93.	BOULEVARD	137.	CANDLE
94.	BOUNTIFUL	138.	CANDLESTICK
95.	BOX OF TISSUES	139.	CANDY CANE
96.	BRA	140.	CANE
97.	BRACELET	141.	CANYON
98.	BRALETTE	142.	CAP
99.	BRANDY	143.	CAPITOL
100.	BRASS	144.	CAPPUCCINO
101.	BRATWURST	145.	CAPRIS
102.	BREAD	146.	CAR
103.	BREEZEWAY	147.	CARAFFE
104.	BREEZY	148.	CARAMEL
105.	BRICK RED	149.	CARDIGAN
106.	BRIDGE	150.	CARIBOU
107.	BRIGHT	151.	CARPET
108.	BRISK	152.	CARROT
109.	BROACH	153.	CASSEROLE
110.	BROCCOLI	154.	CAT
111.	BRONTOSAURUS	155.	CATTLEYA
112.	BRONZE	156.	CATTYWAMPUS
113.	BROWN	157.	CELERY SODA
114.	BRUMOUS	158.	CEREAL
115.	BRUSH	159.	CHAI
116.	BRUSSELS SPROUT	160.	CHAIR
117.	BUBBLE TEA	161.	CHAMBORD
118.	BUGGY	162.	CHAMELEON
119.	BUILDING BLOCKS	163.	CHAMPAGNE
120.	BUREAU	164.	CHANGING
121.	BURGUNDY	165.	CHARCOAL
122.	BUS	166.	CHARTREUSE
123.	BUS STOP	167.	CHECKBOOK
124.	BUSINESS	168.	CHEESE
125.	BUSINESS DISTRICT	169.	CHEESECAKE
126.	BUSYNESS	170.	CHEETAH
127.	BUTTERBEER	171.	CHERRY
128.	BUTTERNUT SQUASH	172.	CHESTNUT
129.	BYPASS	173.	CHICKEN NUGGET
130.	CABBAGE	174.	CHICKEN SOUP
131.	CABINET	175.	CHILDREN
132.	CACTI	176.	CHILI

177.	CHILLY	221.	COOKING
178.	CHIMPANZEE	222.	COOLING
179.	CHIPMUNK	223.	COPPER
180.	CHOCOLATE	224.	CORAL
181.	CHOCOLATE CHIP	225.	CORE
182.	CHOCOLATE MILK	226.	CORKBOARD
183.	CHORES	227.	CORSET
184.	CHROME	228.	COSMOPOLITAN
185.	CHURCH	229.	COUCH
186.	CITY	230.	COUNTY
187.	CLAM	231.	COURTYARD
188.	CLAM DIGGERS	232.	COVERALLS
189.	CLAMMY	233.	COW
190.	CLAY	234.	COYOTE
191.	CLEANING	235.	CRAB
192.	CLEAR	236.	CRACKERS
193.	CLEMENT	237.	CRANBERRY JUICE
194.	CLOCK	238.	CREAM
195.	CLOSET	239.	CREEK
196.	CLOUD	240.	CRICKET
197.	CLOUDLESS	241.	CRISP
198.	CLOUDY	242.	CROCODILE
199.	COAT RACK	243.	CROSSWALK
200.	COCKROACH	244.	CROWD
201.	COCOA POWDER	245.	CUCUMBER
202.	COCONUT	246.	CUDDLING
203.	COCONUT MILK	247.	CUMMERBUND
204.	COCONUT WATER	248.	CUP
205.	COFFEE	249.	CUPOLA
206.	COFFEE CAKE	250.	CURB
207.	COFFEE CUP	251.	CURLING IRON
208.	COFFEE POT	252.	CURRENT
209.	COLA	253.	DAISY DUKES
210.	COLD	254.	DAMASK
211.	COLD BREW COFFEE	255.	DAMP
212.	COMB	256.	DANDILION
213.	COMPUTER MOUSE	257.	DARK
214.	CONCAVE MIRROR	258.	DAY
215.	CONCRETE	259.	DECIDUOUS
216.	CONIFEROUS	260.	DECK
217.	CONSTRUCTION	261.	DECORATION
218.	CONTACTS	262.	DEER
219.	CONTINENT	263.	DEMI
220.	COOKIES	264.	DENIM

265.	DESERT	309.	EASY CHAIR
266.	DESK	310.	EAVES
267.	DETOUR	311.	EBONY
268.	DEWY	312.	EEL
269.	DIET SODA	313.	EGGPLANT
270.	DIM	314.	EGGSHELL
271.	DINING ROOM	315.	ELEPHANT
272.	DIP	316.	ELEVATOR
273.	DIPTHONG	317.	ELK
274.	DIRT	318.	EL
275.	DIRTY MOJITO	319.	EMERALD
276.	DISHES	320.	ESPRESSO
277.	DISHWASHER	321.	EXERCISE ROOM
278.	DISHWATER	322.	EXPRESSWAY
279.	DISMAL	323.	FAÇADE
280.	DODO BIRD	324.	FACTORY
281.	DOG	325.	FAIR
282.	DOLPHIN	326.	FAKE MOUSTACHE
283.	DOME	327.	FALL
284.	DOMESTIC BEER	328.	FAMILY
285.	DONUT SPRINKLE	329.	FAN
286.	DOOR	330.	FATHER
287.	DOWNTOWN	331.	FAUCET
288.	DRAFTY	332.	FENCE
289.	DRAGON	333.	FERRET
290.	DRESS SHOES	334.	FIELD
291.	DRESSER	335.	FILE FOLDER
292.	DRIVE	336.	FIRE HYDRANT
293.	DRIVE-THROUGH	337.	FIRE PIT
294.	DRIVEWAY	338.	FIREFIGHTERS
295.	DRIVWAY	339.	FIREPLACE
296.	DRIZZLING	340.	FISH
297.	DRUMLIN	341.	FISHING POLE
298.	DRY	342.	FLABBERGASTED
299.	DRYER	343.	FLAVORED WATER
300.	DUCK	344.	FLIP FLOPS
301.	DUCK-BILLED PLATYPUS	345.	FLOOR
302.	DULL	346.	FLOWER
303.	EAR BUD	347.	FLOWER BED
304.	EAR OF CORN	348.	FLOWERS
305.	EARL GREY	349.	FLUFFLE
306.	EARRINGS	350.	FLY
307.	EARTHQUAKE	351.	FLYING SQUIRREL
308.	EAST	352.	FOGGY

353.	FOLIAGE	397.	GOWN
354.	FOOT LONG SUB	398.	GRAPE JUICE
355.	FOOTBALL	399.	GRAPEFRUIT
356.	FOREST GREEN	400.	GRAPEFRUIT JUICE
357.	FOUNTAIN	401.	GRASS
358.	FOUNTAIN DRINK	402.	GRASSLAND
359.	FOX	403.	GRAVITY
360.	FOYER	404.	GRAY
361.	FRAGRANT	405.	GREEN
362.	FREEWAY	406.	GREEN TEA
363.	FREEZER	407.	GRAY/GREY
364.	FREEZING	408.	GRILL BRUSH
365.	FRIGID	409.	GUESTS
366.	FROSTED CUPCAKE	410.	GUINEA PIG
367.	FROSTY	411.	GUITAR
368.	FRUITFUL	412.	GUSTY
369.	FUNGUS	413.	HAILING
370.	FURS	414.	HALLWAY
371.	FUSCHIA	415.	HALTER TOP
372.	FUZZY SLIPPERS	416.	HAM
373.	GAMBOGE	417.	HAMSTER
374.	GARAGE	418.	HANDCUFFS
375.	GARBAGE	419.	HAWK
376.	GARGOYLE	420.	HAY BALE
377.	GARLIC BREAD	421.	HAZE
378.	GARTER BELT	422.	HEATER
379.	GAS CAN	423.	HEELS
380.	GATORADE	424.	HEN
381.	GELATO	425.	HIGHLAND
382.	GERBIL	426.	HIGHLIGHTER
383.	GINGER ALE	427.	HILL
384.	GIRAFFE	428.	HIPPOPOTAMUS
385.	GLACIER	429.	HISTORIC
386.	GLARING	430.	HOME PHONE
387.	GLASSES	431.	HOMELESS
388.	GLOOMY	432.	HONEYDEW MELON
389.	GLOVES	433.	HOPE CHEST
390.	GOAT	434.	HORNET
391.	GOLD	435.	HORSE
392.	GOLDENROD	436.	HOT
393.	GOLF BALL	437.	HOT CHOCOLATE
394.	GOLLASHES	438.	HOT CIDER
395.	GORGEOUS	439.	HUMID
396.	GORILLA	440.	HUNTER

441.	HURRICANE	485.	LADYBUG
442.	HYENA	486.	LAKE
443.	ICE CAP	487.	LAMENTABLE
444.	ICED COFFEE	488.	LAMP
445.	ICED TEA	489.	LAND-LOCKED
446.	ICY	490.	LANDSCAPING
447.	IGNITRON	491.	LARGE FRY
448.	IGUANA	492.	LASAGNA
449.	IMPORTED BEER	493.	LATTE
450.	INCLEMENT	494.	LAUNDRY
451.	INCUBATOR	495.	LAVA
452.	INDIGO	496.	LAVENDER
453.	INFUSED WATER	497.	LAWN
454.	INLAND	498.	LEAD PIPE
455.	INSTANT COFFEE	499.	LEASH
456.	INTENSE	500.	L.E.D.
457.	IPHONE ®	501.	LEEKS
458.	IRISH CREAM	502.	LEGGINGS
459.	ISLAND	503.	LEMON
460.	ISTHMUS	504.	LEMONADE
461.	ITALIAN SODA	505.	LEOPARD
462.	IVORY	506.	LETTER OPENER
463.	JACKET	507.	LETTUCE
464.	JACK-IN-THE-BOX	508.	LIGHT
465.	JADE	509.	LIGHT BULB
466.	JAGUAR	510.	LIGHTNING
467.	JASPER	511.	LILAC
468.	JEANS	512.	LIME
469.	JELLY BEAN	513.	LIMEADE
470.	JELLYFISH	514.	LION
471.	JOCKSTRAP	515.	LIPSTICK
472.	KAHLUA	516.	LITTER
473.	KANGAROO	517.	LIVER SAUSAGE
474.	KEFIR	518.	LIZARD
475.	KEY	519.	LOBBY
476.	KEYSTONE	520.	LOBSTER
477.	KITCHEN	521.	LOCK
478.	KIWI	522.	LOCKET
479.	KNEE-HIGHS	523.	LOTION
480.	KNICK KNACKS	524.	LOUSY
481.	KNIFE	525.	LOVE
482.	KOALA	526.	LOWLAND
483.	KOMODO DRAGON	527.	MAGENTA
484.	KOOL-AID	528.	MALL

529.	MALT	573.	MOVIE THEATER POPCORN
530.	MANGO	574.	MUD
531.	MANHATTAN	575.	MUFFIN
532.	MANILLA	576.	MUGGY
533.	MAN-MADE	577.	MULLED WINE
534.	MAP	578.	MUNICIPALITY
535.	MARGARITA	579.	MUSHROOM
536.	MAROON	580.	NATURAL
537.	MARSHMALLOW	581.	NAVY BLUE
538.	MARTINI	582.	NECKLACE
539.	MASHED POTATOES	583.	NECTARINE
540.	MASONRY	584.	NEGLIGEE
541.	MAXI	585.	NEIGHBORHOOD
542.	MELTING	586.	NEIGHBORS
543.	MERLOT	587.	NICKEL
544.	MESA	588.	NIGHT
545.	MICROWAVE	589.	NIGHT CRAWLER
546.	MIDI	590.	NORTH
547.	MIDNIGHT BLUE	591.	NOSE RING
548.	MILD	592.	NOTEBOOK
549.	MILK	593.	NUDE
550.	MILKSHAKE	594.	NYLONS
551.	MINISKIRT	595.	OATMEAL
552.	MINT GREEN	596.	OCEAN
553.	MIRROR	597.	OFFICE
554.	MISTY	598.	OFFICE BUILDING
555.	MITOCHONDRIA *(not midi-chlorean)*	599.	OLD FASHIONED
556.	MITTENS	600.	OLIVE
557.	MIXED DRINK	601.	OPAL
558.	MOCHA	602.	ORANGE
559.	MOIST	603.	ORANGE JUICE
560.	MOJITO	604.	ORANGE SODA
561.	MONKEY	605.	ORANGUTAN
562.	MONUMENT	606.	OVEN RANGE
563.	MOON	607.	OVERCAST
564.	MOOSE	608.	OWL
565.	MORAINE	609.	OYSTER
566.	MOSCOW MULE	610.	PAINT
567.	MOSQUITO	611.	PAJAMAS
568.	MOSS	612.	PANDA
569.	MOTHER	613.	PANTIES
570.	MOUNTAIN	614.	PANTS
571.	MOUSE	615.	PAPERBAG
572.	MOVIE CAMERA	616.	PAPERCLIP

617.	PARAPET	661.	PLATEAU
618.	PARK	662.	PLAYROOM
619.	PARKA	663.	PLAZA
620.	PARKING LOT	664.	PLEASANT
621.	PARKING METER	665.	PLUM
622.	PARKING STRUCTURE	666.	POLAR BEAR
623.	PARKING TICKETS	667.	POLICE
624.	PARKWAY	668.	POMEGRANATE
625.	PARROT	669.	POND
626.	PATE	670.	POPPY SEED
627.	PATIO	671.	PORCALIN
628.	PAVERS	672.	PORCH
629.	PEA	673.	PORCUPINE
630.	PEA GREEN	674.	PORTICO
631.	PEACH	675.	POSTCARD
632.	PEACOCK	676.	POURING
633.	PEAK	677.	PRAIRIE
634.	PEANUT BUTTER	678.	PREDICTABLE
635.	PEBBLE	679.	PRUNE JUICE
636.	PEN	680.	PTERODACTYL
637.	PENCIL	681.	PUCE
638.	PENGUIN	682.	PUMPKIN
639.	PENINSULA	683.	PUMPKIN
640.	PEPPERCORN	684.	PUMPKIN JUICE
641.	PERIWINKLE	685.	PUMPKIN SPICE LATTE
642.	PERSONAL PAN PIZZA	686.	PUMPS
643.	PET FENCE	687.	PURPLE
644.	PETS	688.	PUSH PIN
645.	PEWTER	689.	PUZZLE
646.	PHOTO ALBUMS	690.	QUILL
647.	PICKLE	691.	RACCOON
648.	PICTURE FRAME	692.	RAIN PONCHO
649.	PICTURES	693.	RAINFOREST
650.	PIE	694.	RAINING
651.	PIFFLE	695.	RAINY
652.	PIG	696.	RAMP
653.	PILLAR	697.	RASPBERRY
654.	PILLOW	698.	RAT
655.	PINEAPPLE	699.	RED
656.	PINEAPPLE JUICE	700.	RED LIGHT DISTRICT
657.	PINK	701.	RED WINE
658.	PINT OF ICE CREAM	702.	REED
659.	PIRANHA	703.	REFRESHING
660.	PLANT	704.	REFRIGERATOR

705.	REINDEER		749.	SELTZER WATER
706.	RESISTOR		750.	SEVERE
707.	REVOLVER		751.	SHAPEWEAR
708.	RHINOCEROS		752.	SHARK
709.	RHUBARB		753.	SHAWL
710.	RING		754.	SHEEP
711.	RIVER		755.	SHELF
712.	ROAD		756.	SHELLS
713.	ROCK		757.	SHIRT
714.	ROMAINE LETTUCE		758.	SHOELACE
715.	ROOIBUS TEA		759.	SHORELINE
716.	ROOSTER		760.	SHORTS
717.	ROOTBEER		761.	SHOVEL
718.	ROOTBEER FLOAT		762.	SHOWER
719.	ROPE		763.	SHRIMP
720.	ROSE		764.	SIDEWALK
721.	ROT GUT		765.	SIENNA
722.	ROTTEN		766.	SILVER
723.	ROTUNDA		767.	SINK
724.	ROYAL BLUE		768.	SKIRT
725.	RUBBERS		769.	SKORT
726.	RUM		770.	SKY BLUE
727.	RUM PUNCH		771.	SKYLINE
728.	RURAL		772.	SKYSCRAPER
729.	RUST		773.	SKYWALK
730.	SAKE		774.	SLACKS
731.	SALAMANDER		775.	SLATE
732.	SALT		776.	SLED
733.	SAND		777.	SLEEPING
734.	SANGRIA		778.	SLEETING
735.	SARCOLINE		779.	SLUSHIE
736.	SASSPERILLA		780.	SMALT
737.	SCARF		781.	SMOG
738.	SCARLET		782.	SMOGGY
739.	SCHOOL ZONE		783.	SMOKE
740.	SCORCHING		784.	SMOOTHIE
741.	SCREWDRIVER		785.	SNAKE
742.	SEA		786.	SNOG
743.	SEA GREEN		787.	SNOWING
744.	SEA LEVEL		788.	SNOWY
745.	SEASON		789.	SOCCER BALL
746.	SEASONABLE		790.	SOCKS
747.	SEASONAL		791.	SODA
748.	SEDIMENT		792.	SOUR MILK

11

793.	SOUTH	837.	SUMMER
794.	SPACE	838.	SUN
795.	SPANISH RICE	839.	SUNGLASSES
796.	SPARKLING WATER	840.	SUNNY
797.	SPECK OF DUST	841.	SURFACE STREETS
798.	SPIDER	842.	SUSHI
799.	SPINACH	843.	SUSPENDERS
800.	SPORT COAT	844.	SWAN
801.	SPORTS BRA	845.	SWEATER
802.	SPRING	846.	SWEATS
803.	SPRINKLER	847.	SWEATSHIRT
804.	SQUARE	848.	SWEET PEA
805.	SQUASH BLOSSOM	849.	SWEET POTATO
806.	SQUISHY	850.	SWELTERING
807.	STAINED GLASS	851.	SWIMSUIT
808.	STAMP	852.	SWISS CHARD
809.	STAPLER	853.	SWITCH PLATE
810.	STAR	854.	SYNERGISTIC
811.	STEAMER	855.	TABLE
812.	STEEL	856.	TABLECLOTH
813.	STETHESCOPE	857.	TABLET
814.	STICKY	858.	TACO
815.	STIFLING	859.	TAN
816.	STILL	860.	TANK TOP
817.	STINGRAY	861.	TAP BEER
818.	STINKY	862.	TAPE
819.	STOCKINGS	863.	TAR
820.	STOLE	864.	TARADIDDLE
821.	STONE	865.	TAUPE
822.	STOP SIGN	866.	TAXI
823.	STORM	867.	TELEVISION
824.	STORMING	868.	TEMPERATE
825.	STORMY	869.	TEMPESTUOUS
826.	STOVE	870.	TENNIS SHOES
827.	STRAWBERRY	871.	TEPID
828.	STREAM	872.	TERRIBLE
829.	STREET	873.	TEST TUBE
830.	STREET CLOTHES	874.	THAI CHILI PEPPER
831.	STUFFY	875.	THAWING
832.	SUB-TROPIC	876.	THEATER GLOVES
833.	SUBURBAN	877.	THIMBLE
834.	SUBWAY	878.	THONGS
835.	SUGAR	879.	THREATENING
836.	SULTRY	880.	THROW RUG

881.	THUNDER	925.	UNICORN
882.	TICTAC	926.	UNMENTIONABLES
883.	TIE	927.	UNPREDICTABLE
884.	TIGER	928.	UNSEASONABLE
885.	TIGHTS	929.	UNSTABLE
886.	TITTLE	930.	UPTOWN
887.	TO-DO LIST	931.	URBAN
888.	TOE NAIL	932.	USB CABLE
889.	TOE RING	933.	UTENSILS
890.	TOILET	934.	VALLEY
891.	TOLLWAY	935.	VENISON
892.	TOMATO	936.	VERMILION
893.	TOMATO JUICE	937.	VILLIAGE
894.	TONIC WATER	938.	VIOLENT
895.	TOOLS	939.	VIOLET
896.	TOOTHBRUSH	940.	VIOLIN
897.	TOP HAT	941.	VITAMIN
898.	TOPAZ	942.	VITAMIN WATER
899.	TORNADO	943.	VODKA
900.	TOUCAN	944.	VODKA LEMONADE
901.	TOUPE	945.	VOLCANO
902.	TOWEL	946.	VOLLEYBALL
903.	TOWN	947.	WALL
904.	TOWN HALL	948.	WALLPAPER
905.	TRAFFIC	949.	WARDROBE
906.	TRANQUIL	950.	WARM
907.	TREE	951.	WARMING
908.	TROPICAL	952.	WARM-UPS
909.	TROUSER SOCKS	953.	WASHCLOTH
910.	TROUSERS	954.	WASHER
911.	TRUFFLES	955.	WASP
912.	T-SHIRT	956.	WASSEL
913.	TSUNAMI	957.	WATER
914.	TUNDRA	958.	WATER HEATER
915.	TUNIC	959.	WATER MOCCASIN
916.	TUNNEL	960.	WATERCHESTNUT
917.	TURKEY	961.	WATERMELON
918.	TURQUOISE	962.	WAVE
919.	TUXEDO	963.	WEDGES
920.	TWILIGHT	964.	WEST
921.	TYRANNOSAURUS REX	965.	WET
922.	UMBRELLA	966.	WHALE
923.	UNBEARABLE	967.	WHEAT GRASS
924.	UNDERWARE	968.	WHEEL

969.	WHISKEY	985.	WOOD
970.	WHISTLE	986.	WOODWORK
971.	WHITE	987.	WOOLLY MAMMOTH
972.	WHITE SODA	988.	WORM
973.	WHITE WINE	989.	WRAP
974.	WHITEBOARD	990.	WRAPPING PAPER
975.	WILLIES	991.	WRENCH
976.	WINDLESS	992.	XANDU
977.	WINDOW	993.	YARD
978.	WINDY	994.	YELLOW
979.	WINE GLASS	995.	YELLOW-GREEN
980.	WINTER	996.	YOGA PANTS
981.	WINTER COAT	997.	YOGURT
982.	WINTER WHITE	998.	ZEBRA
983.	WINTRY	999.	ZUCCHINI
984.	WOLF	1000.	ZYGOTE

Food can bring so much to a story. First, it humanizes our characters. They EAT! You know, just like you and I. Did you ever notice how little people in the movies eat? They sit before plates of food. They prepare food. They smell food and maybe even TASTE it, but rarely do you see them fully consume a meal.

I'm not saying that we should walk through counting the fifteen chews per bite that your character has, but it's okay for the people in your stories to really experience their food. Why? Because WE DO. Tastes and smells (which often come together) are powerful senses to which most of us can relate.

Relatability is just the beginning, though!

In writing, food words can also determine:

- **Etiquette** – Does your character break the bread first, or sink his teeth directly into a full baguette?
- **Geographic Location** – The United States Deep South dinner table would look very different from a Northern California meal!
- **Ethnicity** – Avoid stereotypes, but there is reality to being raised in parts of the world where beef is more common, versus seafood, versus dairy and breads, etc.
- **Time of Year** – Is it Crockpot season or grilling season?
- **Weather**–Is your character eating chopped salad on the deck or chili in front of the fireplace?
- **Mood** – You may already know from the 500+ Happenings or 700+ Verbal Emojis books, but words can have temperance and intensity; the same is true for foods.

The following list of 100 alphabetic foods includes the words and a "still-useful" note about each word that may help spark some inspiration for your usage.

STILL USEFUL FOOD	STILL USEFUL NOTE ABOUT FOOD WORD
2-LITER SODA	Hopefully diet or that's way too much sugar for a normal person.
APPLE	One a day keeps the doctor away. Assuming it's raw. Apple pie, apple dumpling, baked apple and apple cobbler don't count.
ARTICHOKE	Makes good dip, but hearts are best.
AVOCADO	Baby starter food and wonderful accompaniment for anything Mexican and sandwiches.
BACON BIT	A sorry excuse for bacon.
BANANA SPLIT	Classic.
BEEF	Dead cow.
BITE-SIZED CANDY BAR	Just the right amount at any given time. Quickest items to disappear from the office candy jar.
BLUEBERRY	Blaubeeren. Used alone or in breakfast, lunch or dinner.
BREAD	Raw toast.
BROCCOLI	Does anyone actually eat the stems? Is that what they're called? Stems?
BRUSSELS SPROUT	Tiny cabbages. Terribly misunderstood.
BUTTERNUT SQUASH	Sweet enough on its own. People really need to stop putting sugar and maple and all that on there.
CABBAGE	Best with corned beef.
CAKE	Yes please.
PEANUT BUTTER	Good source of protein and energy.
CANDY CANE	Classic red and white are best - for eating or hanging on the tree.
SQUASH BLOSSOM	Forget your hesitancies. Stuff it was cheese, batter it up and give it a fry. Very delicious.
CARROT	Eaten by bunnies and people. Come in many colors.
CASSEROLE	Usually cheesy mush.
LIVER SAUSAGE	Leberwurst. Comes in fresh or smoke (braunschweiger). Also rumored to help babies develop into not picky eaters and more willing to try new foods if offered as one of the first table foods. It worked in my family pretty successfully.
CEREAL	Easiest breakfast ever.
CHEESE	More varieties than one can count.
CHEESECAKE	Cheese in dessert form.
CHERRY	Best from Door County. Like blueberries, used alone or in breakfast, lunch or dinner.
CHICKEN NUGGET	Fried units of pressed, shaped, and molded bits of chicken meat. And yet we let our children eat them.

STILL USEFUL FOOD	STILL USEFUL NOTE ABOUT FOOD WORD
CHICKEN SOUP	Best medicine for a cold.
CHILI	Staple fall/winter food. Particularly yummy during football games.
CHOCOLATE CHIP	Chocolate that is in chip form.
COCOA POWDER	Cocoa that is powdered.
COCONUT	Tasty in desserts and drinks.
COFFEE CAKE	Sweet bread for breakfast, eaten (not made) with coffee!
COOKIES	Yes please.
CRAB	Best if eaten shortly after catching.
CRACKERS	A vehicle for getting other foods into the mouth, like dips, peanut butter, other spreads, cheese, salsas, etc.
CUCUMBER	Pairs well with melon.
DIP	The reason crackers exist.
MUFFIN	Naked and somewhat healthier cupcake.
DONUT SPRINKLE	Makes the donuts classy.
EAR OF CORN	Single unit of corn containing multiple kernels.
EGGPLANT	Mostly used in Italian preparations/dished.
FOOT LONG SUB	A submarine sandwich approximately 12 inches long give or take. Usually take. And by 1-2 inches.
FROSTED CUPCAKE	Bliss.
GARLIC BREAD	Salty, seasoned, buttery toast.
GELATO	Italian ice cream.
GRAPEFRUIT	Citrus fruit with no grape-like flavor.
HAM	Smoked cut of pig.
HONEYDEW MELON	Green cantaloupe with a slightly different flavor.
JELLY BEAN	Neither jelly, nor a bean.
LARGE FRY	More than one person should eat.
LASAGNA	Hearty, heavy, layered Italian dish that can accommodate almost any vegetable, and any large family or meal donation.
LEEKS	Great roasted.
LEMON	Yellow citrus fruit.
LETTUCE	Basically, the foundation of all salads.
LOBSTER	Steak of the ocean.
MANGO	Can be eaten raw or used in drinks. Alcoholic or not.
MARSHMALLOW	Fluffy sweet that melts into napalm.
MOVIE THEATER POPCORN	One of the best forms of junk food ever. Providing something remotely resembling real butter is used. Must include copious amounts of butter and salt.

STILL USEFUL FOOD	STILL USEFUL NOTE ABOUT FOOD WORD
MUSHROOM	Edible fungus.
BRATWURST	Also simply called a "brat."
NECTARINE	Smooth peach.
PEPPERCORN	Ground and used to season food.
MASHED POTATOES	Thanksgiving staple
PERSONAL PAN PIZZA	What you order when you have really bizarre taste in pizza toppings. Like mushroom, green pepper and pineapple.
PICKLE	A good accompaniment to sandwiches or satisfying snack for a pregnant lady.
PIE	Fruit done up as a dessert.
KIWI	Fuzzy fruit with a seedy green interior.
PINEAPPLE	Eat alone, in fruit salad, cooked, or use in drinks.
PINT OF ICE CREAM	Single serving for most men, women going through a break-up and children with no concept of portion control
PLUM	Baked into Christmas pies.
POMEGRANATE	Considered by some to be an aphrodisiac
POPPY SEED	Don't eat too many before a drug test.
PATE	Squished up, almost liquefied spreadable meat.
PUMPKIN	Typically baked into a pie for thanksgiving, but can be used in other desserts and even prepared as a side-dish like squash.
RASPBERRY	Small red berries having multiple seeds.
RHUBARB	Can cut down on the bitter flavor by soaking in buttermilk prior to use or using buttermilk in the batter if baking into a coffee cake/muffin/etc.
ROMAINE LETTUCE	Basically, the foundation of all salads.
WATERCHESTNUT	Staple in Chinese food. Wrapped in bacon and baked and served as an appetizer.
SALT	What you put on all vegetable to disguise taste.
SHRIMP	Can be pretty big.
SPANISH RICE	Rice dressed up with Spanish seasonings and flavors
SPINACH	The foundation of salads when you're trying to be healthier than salad.
STRAWBERRY	Red berries having multiple seeds.

STILL USEFUL FOOD	STILL USEFUL NOTE ABOUT FOOD WORD
SUGAR	Used in combination with butter to provide mechanical leavening in baking.
SUSHI	Raw fish.
SWEET PEA	Peas. That are sweet.
SWEET POTATO	Potatoes. That are sweet.
SWISS CHARD	Not as popular green, but good cooked up with butter and bacon.
THAI CHILI PEPPER	Spicy pepper.
TACO	To be eaten on Tuesdays. Because Taco Tuesday.
TICTAC	tiny breath mint
TOMATO	Knowledge is knowing a tomato is a fruit. Wisdom is not putting it in a fruit salad. Philosophy is wondering if that means ketchup is a smoothie. *(Author unknown)*
TRUFFLES	Very expensive mushrooms or very luxurious chocolate bonbon
TURKEY	Bird eaten at thanksgiving
VENISON	Deer meat; ever wonder where we get the words that correspond with the meats that come from the animals?
WATERMELON	Giant fruit with a green rind and pink flesh.
WHEAT GRASS	What people put in a drink to be healthy.
WRAP	Sandwich in a thin flexible shell instead of on bread
YOGURT	U.S., Australian, and Greek varieties all have different consistencies.
ZUCCHINI	Looks like a cucumber, behaves like a squash.

Word

Word Play!

Play

Word Play!

Word

Play

Play

Word

Word Play!

WORD PLAY . . . YOUR Food Words and Notes

Time to play! What foods can you think of and notes that tell you about the food, what the food can bring to mind for a character, how the food can change a scene, or just a note about why the food is still useful in your writing?

FOOD WORD	STILL USEFUL FOOD WORD NOTE (TO SELF)

It's consumption, so of course putting beverages into your scenes and characterizations can do a lot of the same things as food, in terms of creating relatability, etiquette, geographic location, ethnicity, time of year, weather, and mood; BUT – they do something else, too. They allow your characters . . . and therefore your readers . . . to take a breath!

Have you ever noticed the sheer noise, activity, and pace of our world? We don't even stop to breathe when we're eating. We chew on and on while babbling, either "delicately" by covering our mouth, or . . . well . . . you know . . . the whole etiquette (or lack thereof) thing that could have your character garbage mouthing through a soap box speech.

Seriously!

Are we so consumed by the desire to be heard that we don't stop speaking while in the act of consuming?

BUT . . .

With drinking, unlike eating, your character must pause, sip . . . or gulp . . . or pour . . . or swish, then close, then swallow, and usually even take an extra beat before spewing forth once more. (Although, if the drinking is alcohol, there is sometimes simultaneous spewing, but of a different kind.) Of course, at that point, you may be addressing the other thing beverage can bring into play, such as addictions and vices: caffeine every morning, wine every evening, manhattans and cosmos (you just thought of gender, by the way!) to excess, and so on.

The following list of 100 alphabetic beverages includes the words and a "still-useful" note about each word that may help spark some inspiration for your usage. I admit we're a bit irreverent at times; get used to it . . . or try any number of the suggestions on this list while you work your way through these still useful words!

STILL USEFUL BEVERAGE	STILL USEFUL NOTE ABOUT BEVERAGE WORD
ABSINTH	A very, very, very alcoholic beverage flavored with anise.
ALE	Full-bodied beer.
AMARETTO	Almond flavored liqueur and my publisher's favorite drink.
APPLE CIDER	Raw apple juice.
APPLE JUICE	Juice . . . from apples.
APPLETINI	Martini with an apple flair and the classic "girl's drink".
BAHAMA MAMA	Orange and yellow alcoholic drink made with rum, pineapple juice, orange juice and coconut flavor.
BEER	Alcoholic beverage based on fermented starches.
BLACK TEA	Tea from black tea leaves.
BLUSH WINE	A fruitier, gentler wine . . . that your grandmother drinks.
BRANDY	Winter liqueur derived from grapes.
BUBBLE TEA	AKA boba juice; tea-based drink with fun tapioca balls.
BUTTERBEER	Nonalcoholic drink popularized by Harry Potter.
CAPPUCCINO	Espresso and milk drink.
CELERY SODA	Carbonated celery-flavored beverage popular in Hong Kong.
CHAI	A type of spiced tea.
CHAMBORD	Raspberry liqueur.
CHOCOLATE MILK	A sorry excuse for milk . . . in my humble opinion.
COCONUT MILK	Sort of coconut tea - made by soaking coconut flesh in water and squeezing it out.
COCONUT WATER	Unlike coconut milk, this is the actual liquid found in coconuts (and nearly impossible to get to)!
COFFEE	Usually caffeinated beverage brewed from coffee beans – and tastes basically the same no matter how it's brewed these days.
COLA	Dark soda.
COLD BREW COFFEE	Coffee that is brewed cold that some people say tastes better than normal coffee brewed normally and then made cold.
COSMOPOLITAN	Pinkish cranberry martini made popular by Sex and the City.
CRANBERRY JUICE	Juice . . . from cranberries.
DIET SODA	Carbonated beverage that is lower in calories, sugar, or both as compared to a non-diet version . . . but still horrible for you.

STILL USEFUL BEVERAGE	STILL USEFUL NOTE ABOUT BEVERAGE WORD
DIRTY MOJITO	Mojito made with brown sugar.
DOMESTIC BEER	Beer from the country where you live.
EARL GREY	Black tea flavored with bergamot and drank "HOT" by Star Trek's Captain Picard.
ESPRESSO	Thick, strong, black coffee with grounds that could be read by Harry Potter's Professor Trelawney . . . THE GRIM!
FLAVORED WATER	Water having a flavor but no added calories . . . modern marvels.
FOUNTAIN DRINK	Soda on tap.
GATORADE	A particular type of sports drink with electrolytes (which basically means salt) and energy restoration (which basically means sugar).
GINGER ALE	Carbonated drink flavored with ginger - good for upset stomachs.
GRAPE JUICE	Juice . . . from grapes.
GRAPEFRUIT JUICE	Juice . . . from grapefruit.
GREEN TEA	Tea from green leaves.
HOT CHOCOLATE	A warm chocolate beverage made with milk, cream, chocolate and usually sweetener . . . or dried powder, but the earlier is much better!
HOT CIDER	Warmed, pressed, raw apple beverage, sometimes with added spices.
ICED COFFEE	Coffee . . . over ice.
ICED TEA	Tea . . . on ice.
IMPORTED BEER	Beer from any location you are not.
INFUSED WATER	Water in which fruits and/or vegetables have been soaked for the purpose of transferring some of the taste of the fruit/vegetable into the water.
INSTANT COFFEE	Supposedly coffee-flavored granules which dissolve in hot water . . . I don't trust it!
IRISH CREAM	Cream liqueur - good for spicing coffee, or hot chocolate, or your love life.
ITALIAN SODA	Carbonated water flavored with syrup.
KAHLUA	Coffee flavored liqueur – two vices in one drink. Yum.
KEFIR	Fermented yogurt beverage.
KOOL-AID	Oooh yeah.
LATTE	Espresso and steamed milk; a foamless cappuccino.
LEMONADE	What you make when life gives you lemons.
LIMEADE	What you make when life, apparently, gives you limes.
MALT	MALT= <milk + ice cream + malt powder + 1950 + summer>

STILL USEFUL BEVERAGE	STILL USEFUL NOTE ABOUT BEVERAGE WORD
MANHATTAN	Cocktail made with whiskey, vermouth, bitters, and cherry juice.
MARGARITA	On the rocks is a real margarita. Blended is just an adult slushie.
MARTINI	Classic cocktail of gin & vermouth, that today serves as a base for flavor experimentation.
MILK	Juice . . . from a cow.
MILKSHAKE	Milk + ice cream.
MIXED DRINK	Can be shaken or stirred.
MOCHA	Chocolate latte.
MOJITO	Rum, sugar, lime juice, soda water, and mint.
MOSCOW MULE	Cocktail made with vodka, ginger beer and lime juice served in a copper mug.
MULLED WINE	Wine warmed up with various spices and sometimes oranges.
OLD FASHIONED	Cocktail made with whiskey or brandy poured over muddled bitters and sometimes orange zest.
ORANGE JUICE	Juice . . . from oranges
ORANGE SODA	Carbonated orange-flavored beverage staple of computer hacking geniuses (at least on television).
PINEAPPLE JUICE	Juice . . . from pineapple
PRUNE JUICE	What old people drink to stay . . . *regular*.
PUMPKIN JUICE	Chilled pumpkin-based juice popularized by Harry Potter.
PUMPKIN SPICE LATTE	A warmed beverage containing some sort of coffee and sweet pumpkin spice flavored syrup and milk that is a staple in the teen/20/30-age female diet unless you actually like coffee.
RED WINE	Wine . . . that is red.
ROOIBUS TEA	Red, highly caffeinated tea.
ROOTBEER	Carbonated beverage made from sassafras and sarsaparilla.
ROOTBEER FLOAT	Root beer with ice cream floating in it and making all sorts of extra foamy bubbles.
ROT GUT	Cheap, poor quality, sometimes poisonous alcohol.
RUM	Sugarcane-based distilled alcohol.
RUM PUNCH	A fruity punch spiked with rum, typically served in tropical locations and the exact fruit combinations can vary by region.
SAKE	Very strong rice wine popular in Japan.

STILL USEFUL BEVERAGE	STILL USEFUL NOTE ABOUT BEVERAGE WORD
SANGRIA	Wine plus fruit salad . . . that you drink . . . then chew.
SASPERILLA	Like root beer but only made from sarsaparilla.
SCREWDRIVER	Orange juice + vodka.
SELTZER WATER	Carbonated water.
SLUSHIE	Finely crushed ice flavored with a sweet syrup.
SMOOTHIE	Blended fruit drink usually containing dairy.
SODA	Flavored carbonated beverage.
SOUR MILK	Expired milk . . .or a bad attitude.
SPARKLING WATER	Carbonated water, usually having a slight flavor.
SQUISHY	A slushie enjoyed at Universal Studios and purchased from the Kwik-e mart.
STEAMER	Warmed milk, usually flavored with a flavored syrup.
TAP BEER	Beer from a keg.
TOMATO JUICE	Juice . . . from tomato (and typically including various seasonings).
TONIC WATER	Carbonated water with quinine . . . or medicine if it's like 1860 and you sell snake oil.
VITAMIN WATER	Water enriched with vitamins and usually flavored.
VODKA	Distilled alcohol usually made from fermented potatoes.
VODKA LEMONADE	When life gives you lemons . . . and vodka
WASSEL	Hot mulled cider, wine, or punch containing alcohol.
WATER	H2O
WHISKEY	Fermented grain mash-based distilled alcohol.
WHITE SODA	Not dark soda; usually a lemon or lime flavor.
WHITE WINE	Wine . . . that is white.

Word
Word Play!
Play
Word Play!
Word
Play
Play

Word
Word Play!

WORD PLAY . . . YOUR Beverage Words and Notes

Time to play! What beverages can you think of and notes that tell you about the beverage, what the beverage can bring to mind for a character, how the beverage can change a scene, or just a note about why the beverage is still useful in your writing?

BEVERAGE WORD	STILL USEFUL BEVERAGE WORD NOTE (TO SELF)

100 Still Useful Random Objects

Try keeping a list someday of every plain old object you come into contact with. More than likely, if you try really, really hard, you'll maybe name ten percent of them.

On the whole, we are very visual people; we take in the PICTURES around us. In the most literal sense, we are seeing the forests, and not the trees. These sweeping pictures are only part of our world, though. We have four other physical senses, plus the added concept of how different things in our world affect us, sometimes to the point of completely eschewing the reality of the original picture!

Our jobs as writers are to PUT the 1000 words to each of the pictures, not just to talk about the big pictures.

Random objects are everywhere and they humanize characters. From toothbrushes to recycle bins, a random object has just as much chance to make a scene come to life as the people who are using or coming into contact with it.

The following list of 100 alphabetic random objects includes the words and a "still-useful" note about each word that may help spark some inspiration for your usage.

STILL USEFUL RANDOM OBJECT	STILL USEFUL NOTE ABOUT RANDOM OBJECT
ACORN	Not haycorns, okay?
ADVIL ®	Not Tylenol . . . or aspirin . . . or Aleve.
ALARM CLOCK	Supposed to wake you up on time; in reality, a reminder of how to use your "snooze" button.
BABY DOLL	A doll resembling a baby and kind of creepy if you still collect them as an adult.
BALLOON	Flexible foil or plastic sack which is expanded/firmed by filling it with gas. Just don't release 99 balloons of red color or you will start World War III.
BARRETTE	Hair clip.
BASEBALL	Refers to a sport or the actual ball used in the sport.
BASKET	Open-ended container of braided material.
BIRD BATH	Pool of water left out for birds to sit in.
BLANKET	Sheet of fabric used to stay warm.
BOBBER	Float on a fishing line to keep a hook at a certain depth; mistaken by children everywhere as a Pokémon trap.
BOX OF TISSUES	Or just an empty box you find everytime you look for a tissue.
BRUSH	Not a comb.
BUILDING BLOCKS	Despite the name, can be almost any shape.
CANDLE	Wax stick with a wick; best when scented or topping a birthday cake!
CANDLESTICK	Decorative support for holding a candle and preventing melted wax from dripping on a surface . . . or a murder weapon.
CARAFFE	Portable coffee pot for refilling the coffee cup.
CHECKBOOK	Obsolete.
CLOCK	Annoying ticking thing that tells you you're late.
COAT RACK	For hanging sweaters, purses, keys, shoes, bags, backpacks, scarves, hats, and sacks . . . until there is no longer any actual room for coats.
COFFEE CUP	Handheld basin for holding coffee or just feeling in your hands, especially when it's really cold outside.
COMB	Not a brush.
COMPUTER MOUSE	Oval-ish device that you use when your computer isn't a touch screen and you don't have a touch pad . . . becoming obsolete.

STILL USEFUL RANDOM OBJECT	STILL USEFUL NOTE ABOUT RANDOM OBJECT
CONCAVE MIRROR	Mirror with a reflecting surface that curves inward - like a cave.
CORKBOARD	Board made of cork; ancestor to Pinterest.
CURLING IRON	A hot rod women use to style hair; *who started that whack trend???*
EAR BUD	Headphones that fit in your ear, but rarely feel right.
FAKE MOUSTACHE	A toupee . . . for your lip.
FAN	A person very passionate about something or a multi-bladed structure which rotates to provide cooling.
FILE FOLDER	Good for organizing papers or digital files.
FISHING POLE	Pole with a hook at the end to catch fish.
FOOTBALL	Refers to a sport or the actual ball used in the sport.
GAS CAN	Can . . . for gas.
GLASSES	Lenses worn in front of the eye to improve vision; a fashion statement for some – an annoyance for others.
GOLF BALL	Dimpled ball used in golfing; contain 500 dimples . . . like your arms and neck in the middle of a scary scene in a movie.
GRILL BRUSH	Brush for cleaning crud off a grill (if burning it off doesn't work, first).
GUITAR	Stringed instrument that, according to reports, makes men instantly 50% hotter when they play it.
HANDCUFFS	Hand restraining devices . . . unless you break your own thumb.
HAY BALE	Organized, tightly compacted pile of hay in a cubical or cylindrical shape.
HIGHLIGHTER	Colorful markers or pen that, well, color or mark-up text for call-out purposes, resulting in either irreparable book damage or a book well-loved depending on who you ask.
HOPE CHEST	A box that's supposed to be filled with things to help you toward all those things you hope for, but in reality is usually used for sheets and blankets and that's a pretty low hope-bar.
IGNITRON	A rectifier.
INCUBATOR	For growing baby chicks.
IPHONE ®	Portable phone made by Apple, rereleased annually with a new feature to make grown men wait in lines not experienced since the release of the first Star Wars series, and typically sold with a cord that is two inches short of anywhere you'd like to plug it in.

STILL USEFUL RANDOM OBJECT	STILL USEFUL NOTE ABOUT RANDOM OBJECT
JACK-IN-THE-BOX	Who the heck invented this scary as heck toy for babies and creepy concept for a haunted house room?! It's also a restaurant . . . not nearly as frightening.
KNIFE	Sharp blade . . . or a murder weapon.
LAMP	Electric light that stands on the floor, or a desk, or a table, or—in "The Christmas Story"—on one leg.
LEAD PIPE	Segment of pipe made out of lead . . . or a murder weapon.
LEASH	Harness for an animal or, nowadays, small child (*the latter said with a cringe*).
L.E.D.	Light emitting diode. (Um . . . a light bulb . . . but that uses up a lot less energy.
LETTER OPENER	Sharp object for opening letters.
LIGHT BULB	Glass bulb with a filament that glows when current passes through it.
LIPSTICK	Tint stick for lips.
LOCKET	Jewelry item usually hiding something of sentimental value.
LOTION	Skin moisturizer.
MAP	Visual representation of an area usually provided in an overhead view and with an emphasis on relative locations of certain features (e.g., streets, landmarks, bodies of water, and points of interest) to one another.
MOVIE CAMERA	Camera for taking movies, some of them still use this quickly disappearing medium of "film"!
NOTEBOOK	Book . . . for notes.
PAPERBAG	Bag . . . made of paper.
PAPERCLIP	Clip . . . for papers; or links for a child's crafted necklace for Mother's Day.
PEN	Ink-containing stick for writing.
PENCIL	Lead (or probably graphite) containing stick for writing.
PICTURE FRAME	Display for a picture.
POSTCARD	Cheaper to mail than a letter.
PUSH PIN	Holds papers to your antique Pinterest account.
PUZZLE	Mind-challenging game or perfectly good, cardboard-backed picture cut into small, interlocking pieces to be put back together.
QUILL	Fancy, feathered, writing implement.

STILL USEFUL RANDOM OBJECT	STILL USEFUL NOTE ABOUT RANDOM OBJECT
REED	Plant or somewhat flexible structure designed to vibrate against another surface . . . usually an instrument's mouthpiece.
RESISTOR	Components that reduce current flow.
REVOLVER	Also called a gun, pistol, firearm or ballistic device . . . or a murder weapon when held by a murderous person.
ROPE	Fibrous length of material . . . or a murder weapon.
SHOELACE	For tying shoes . . . probably not strong enough to murder.
SHOVEL	Tool used to remove dirt or debris . . . or, well, you get the idea.
SLED	Mode of transportation, or of fun, typically in winter.
SOCCER BALL	Ball used in playing soccer.
SPECK OF DUST	Usually made of dead skin cells. Yep. Not kidding.
SPRINKLER	Device that releases gentle streams or drops of water, unless somebody bends it into a kink first, before it flows; then, it's a device that releases a face-ripping, frozen explosion of water.
STAMP	Rubber pattern covered with ink and pressed on paper. Or a sticker provided by the post office and placed on a letter or parcel to prove someone paid for the item to ship.
STAPLER	Used to connect two pieces of paper; hurts a lot more when unintentionally used to connect two tips of fingers.
STETHESCOPE	Listens to your heart even if you don't.
STOP SIGN	In the US, an octagonal sign with a red background and white letters. In some neighborhoods, it just means "roll slowly".
SUNGLASSES	Lenses worn in front of the eye to reduce glare or create sexy raccoon striped sunburn after a day at the beach.
TABLET	Can refer to a small computer, a form of a drug or pill, or a pad of paper.
TAPE	It's a big family: duct, measuring, masking, painters', scotch, packaging, medical, and cassette (just kidding; there's no such thing as a cassette tape!)
TEST TUBE	Vial . . . not vile.
THIMBLE	Protective sleeve for a thumb or other finger usually made of metal, china or glass. Other uses: a kiss.

STILL USEFUL RANDOM OBJECT	STILL USEFUL NOTE ABOUT RANDOM OBJECT
TOE NAIL	Protective almost exoskeleton covering the tips of toes.
TOOTHBRUSH	Should be changed at least every three months.
TOUPE	Just, no.
UMBRELLA	Keeps the rain off. Unless you are in an urban location with buildings forming wind tunnels. Then useless - don't even try. Can also refer to the mode of transportation preferred by Mary Poppins.
USB CABLE	Universal Serial Bus cable. (Now, you know.)
VIOLIN	Stringed instrument played by Sherlock Holmes.
VITAMIN	Health pill with all the nutrients you should get from your food.
VOLLEYBALL	Can refer to the sport or the actual ball used in the sport.
WHEEL	Invented by the cavemen and gained instant popularity. Number one used gadget since and of all-time. *"Must have! FIVE STARS!" ~Your Pet Hamster*
WHISTLE	Device which makes a noise when air passes through or over it.
WHITEBOARD	Board . . . that is white. Or, more specifically, a dry-erase board.
WINE GLASS	Glass for holding wine. In other words, the presence of wine instantly transforms the coffee mug into a wine glass.
WRAPPING PAPER	Paper used to conceal the contents of a gift.
WRENCH	Tool . . . or murder weapon.

Word
Word Play!
Play
Word Play!
Word
Play
Play

Word
WORD PLAY!

WORD PLAY . . . YOUR Random Object Words and Notes

Time to play! What random objects can you think of and notes that tell you about the random objects, what the random objects can bring to mind for a character or in your journaling, how the random objects can change a scene, or just a note about why the random object is still useful in your writing?

RANDOM OBJECT WORD	STILL USEFUL RANDOM OBJECT NOTE (TO SELF)

100 Still Useful Weather Words

Weather is so much fun to write. It brings out all the feels!

Obviously, it's an indicator of the season; or, it directly works in contrast to the season, like a warm, Wisconsin Christmas. (It's happened before!)

Weather can also create mood, foreshadow, parallels, cycles, emotional responses, and so much more!

Weather can be used ironically with a hurricane in the middle of a beautiful wedding, or as an intensifier, like a much anticipated fistfight in the middle of a heat wave.

In your journaling, it touches memory. In your dreams, it touches hopes and fears.

With all of the uses for weather words in writing of all kinds, shouldn't you have at least as many of those words to use?

STILL USEFUL WEATHER WORD	STILL USEFUL NOTE ABOUT WEATHER WORD
ARID	Very dry.
BALMY	Pleasantly nice outside and a little warm . . . a touch too humid for some northerners.
BEAUTIFUL	Type of weather is in the eyes, hands, wardrobe of the beholder.
BLEAK	A bitter-type cold experienced during winter in locations away from the equator and associated with general grayness/greyness.
BLINDING	Used to describe situations when the sun is too bright or positioned in the sky to reflect off the landscape and hinder visibility.
BLUE	A clear sky . . . or a dismal day. Food for thought.
BLUSTERY	Good piglet-flying weather.
BREEZY	Kinda windy, but not very.
BRIGHT	Sunny.
BRISK	Cool, usually fall weather
BRUMOUS	Foggy.
BUGGY	Weather suitable for lots of bugs and insects to be out, usually involving an unpleasant amount of humidity.
CALM	Stable weather . . . or a facade of stability coming before a big storm.
CHANGING	If you live near a sizable body of water, changing is a daily occurrence.
CHILLY	Not cold, but not comfortable. Sweater weather!
CLAMMY	Cool dampness . . . blekch!
CLEAR	I can see the sky!
CLEMENT	Mild weather.
CLOUDLESS	No clouds - usually a sign of high pressure. It could change quickly! (See "changing".)
CLOUDY	Lots of clouds and possible erasure of the "blue" in the sky.
COLD	A temperature lower than what one is presently dressed to accommodate. In Southern California, around 50 degrees Fahrenheit, in the Northern States, below 30 degrees. Also, a cold summer day is typically warmer than a warm winter day . . . so there!
COOLING	Decreasing in temperature.

STILL USEFUL WEATHER WORD	STILL USEFUL NOTE ABOUT WEATHER WORD
CRISP	Pleasantly sharp in a cool sort of way.
DAMP	Moist. Did you just cringe? Get over it! It's just a WORD (See "Moist")!
DARK	Cloudy, stormy, no sunshine . . . or, just night.
DEWY	Sparkling beads of condensation on the grass caused by the rising of the warming sun into a cool crisp morning. (Breathe in . . . breathe out.)
DIM	Not quite dark; not light enough.
DISMAL	Sleeping weather. Cuddle under the covers weather. Hide from the world weather. Hot chocolate, reading, and fireplace weather.
DRAFTY	Windy, with wind of a different temperature (usually cooler) than the air.
DRIZZLING	Light not-frozen precipitation.
DRY	Very low humidity.
DULL	Typically refers to dark, dreary, cloudy weather, but can also mean inactive (not storming) weather.
FAIR	Good.
FOGGY	Pea-soup; low-hanging clouds; nice October, or Halloween ambiance.
FREEZING	Below 32F. Unless your circulation stinks. Then freezing is a relative term based on whether or not you need to put on a sweater.
FRIGID	Very cold; more than chilly. The windows are frosted over.
FROSTY	State of having moisture in the air freeze in a light layer over a surface. Kills the plants for the year, or can prevent them from growing if you plant too soon.
GLARING	Blinding in a reflective sort of way.
GLOOMY	Weather characterized by a lot of gray/grey, overcast, threatened rain type feeling.
GORGEOUS	Typically meaning warm, clear, and sunny weather, but can vary by person and by season.
GRAY	Or GREY. Can be smoggy, foggy, or cloudy.
GUSTY	Windy, but not continually windy; rather it is bursts of wind that tend to have a high velocity.
HAILING	Precipitating frozen ice balls that destroy roofs and cars.

STILL USEFUL WEATHER WORD	STILL USEFUL NOTE ABOUT WEATHER WORD
HOT	More than warm relative to a desired or planned for temperature.
HUMID	Damp, moist, wet, and oppressive. Can happen at any time of year, but is typically associated with hot, summer temperatures.
ICY	Freezing conditions on roads covered with frozen water.
INCLEMENT	Bad.
INTENSE	Extreme, but not always bad.
LAMENTABLE	Unsatisfactory and not for a given purpose.
LOUSY	Terrible, bad, horrible, awful.
MELTING	Warming. Great for the spirit; bad for the basement.
MILD	Fair, seasonal, unchanging.
MISTY	Something between foggy and drizzling.
MOIST	Rated one of the worst words in the English language along with secrete, glandular, orifice, and pituitary. Nonetheless, it's how everybody wants their cake!
MUGGY	Hot and humid.
OVERCAST	Cloudy.
PLEASANT	Nice.
POURING	Raining cats and dogs. (Or, frogs if you're stuck in the Medieval Era.)
PREDICTABLE	The weather actually resembles what the weatherman said on the news this morning or last night!
RAINING	Precipitating liquid water.
RAINY	A holding pattern of rain.
REFRESHING	Changed-up, new; or spring-like weather.
ROTTEN	Bad, terrible, or stagnant weather.
SCORCHING	Sizzling, sweltering, hot, blistering.
SEASONABLE	May not be enjoyable, but it's in line with the averages that are usual for the time of year.
SEASONAL	See "Seasonal", but some people prefer "Seasonal" as a word.
SEVERE	Inclement, school-cancelling weather.
SLEETING	Precipitating partially frozen partially liquid water . . . blekch!
SMOGGY	Polluted fog.
SNOWING	Precipitating fluffy frozen water . . . finally pretty.
SNOWY	A holding pattern of snow.

STILL USEFUL WEATHER WORD	STILL USEFUL NOTE ABOUT WEATHER WORD
STICKY	Humid, clingy, closed-in, and heavy with heat
STIFLING	Holding pattern of heat and humidity making the air feel suffocating.
STILL	Calm.
STORMING	Raging.
STORMY	Holding pattern of storms of any type.
STUFFY	Stale.
SULTRY	Hot and humid.
SUNNY	Cloudless, or partially cloudy, but with more open sky showing than not.
SWELTERING	Sizzling, scorching, hot, sunny.
TEMPERATE	Mild temperatures.
TEMPESTUOUS	Stormy . . . but a lot more fun to say!
TEPID	Room temperature . . . blah.
TERRIBLE	Lousy.
THAWING	Warming from freezing.
THREATENING	Risk of inclement weather; looming inclement weather.
TRANQUIL	Peaceful, calm, serene.
TROPICAL	Mimicking the tropics.
UNBEARABLE	Too extreme in one way or another to be pleasant (too hot, too cold, too wet, too dry).
UNPREDICTABLE	Unstable.
UNSEASONABLE	Unusual for a season.
UNSTABLE	Volatile.
VIOLENT	Stormy, inclement.
WARM	Not hot, but hotter than cool.
BLISTERING	So hot it feels like your skin is cooking just from being outside.
WARMING	Increasing in temperature.

STILL USEFUL WEATHER WORD	STILL USEFUL NOTE ABOUT WEATHER WORD
WET	Damp, humid, raining, precipitating, or MOIST (oh yes I did).
WINDLESS	Calm.
WINDY	Breezy, blustery.
WINTRY	Seasonal for winter, but usually referred to in northern latitudes, meaning snow and cold.

Word
Word Play!

Play
Word Play!

Word

Play
Play

Word
WORD PLAY!

50

WORD PLAY . . . YOUR Weather Words and Notes

Time to play! What weather words can you think of and notes that tell you about the weather words, what the weather word can bring to mind for a character, how the weather words can change a scene, or just a note about why a weather word is still useful in your writing? Also, consider specific types of storms and weather-related incidents from tornadoes, to blizzards, to hurricanes, and beyond.

WEATHER WORD	STILL USEFUL WEATHER WORD NOTE (TO SELF)

51

100 Still Useful Color Words

From the time we read Dr. Seuss's *"Many Colored Days"* as children, we start tying color to emotion.

EVERY word in the Still Useful Word List can be further clarified, detailed, punctuated, punched up, and specified through COLOR.

Forget fifty shades of grey when you can have fifty (or a hundred) colors with fifty (or a hundred) shades apiece. And you don't even have to be tied up to learn them. You just need to keep reading.

STILL USEFUL COLOR WORD	STILL USEFUL NOTE ABOUT COLOR WORD
AQUAMARINE	A rich blue-green, but somehow more magical sounding; like a clean and clear body of water.
AUBERGINE	Brown-purple; who knew those colors had a combo name?!
AUBURN	Reddish brown, usually used as a hair color term . . . the tamer redhead; a fancy way to say your hair is brown but you want to be a ginger.
BEIGE	The interior of your grandma's car, more than likely; not brown, not cream, and not tan.
BISQUE	Like a biscuit!
BLACK	The absence of all light; or like night, and sheep, and really rich, delicious, South American coffee.
BLOOD	Usually red, but - in reality - blue in the body and deep brown after out for too long.
BLUE	General term used to describe the color of sky and clean water bodies and sadness; technically, any visible light between 450-495 *wavelengths in nanometers*, or *nm*.
BRASS	A gold-color common to musical instruments and bed frames made in the 1980s.
BRICK RED	Burnt reddish orange, probably because bricks are made by burning reddish orange clay; classic crayon color.
BRONZE	Metallic brown.
BROWN	Combination of all primary colors.
BURGUNDY	Deep purple red, like the wine it's named for; located somewhere around #43302E.
CADET	Up for debate whether this is a blue or a gray/grey, color found at #91A3B0.
CARAMEL	Somewhere between yellow and brown and orange, but somehow appetizing and not disgusting looking, unlike baby poop which is a similar color.
CATTLEYA	Kind of like lavender. Sure. We'll go with that.
CHAMPAGNE	Such a light yellow, it's almost clear . . . *almost*.
CHARCOAL	Darkest gray/grey to almost black.
CHARTREUSE	Yellow-green, named for a liqueur used by monks – really!
CHESTNUT	Deep brown, like a deer's eye; popular color for hair dye.

STILL USEFUL COLOR WORD	STILL USEFUL NOTE ABOUT COLOR WORD
CHOCOLATE	A medium brown, although for baking, darker is better.
CHROME	Bright silver; usually a coating.
COFFEE	Dark brown . . . almost black.
COPPER	If gold and rust had an illegitimate child; unless it's very old copper - then it's as if green and white had a child.
CORAL	Somewhere between pink and orange even though coral, itself, comes in a rainbow of colors.
CREAM	Mostly white, with a touch of beige; generally used to refer to any off-white color in the brownish/yellow direction, while still remaining pastel.
DAMASK	A pinkish, grayish/greyish red; can be confused with dusty rose.
DANDELION	Brightest yellow and if it reflects under your chin, you probably like butter.
DENIM	Uneven, rich, blue color often speckled with white and gray/grey.
DISHWATER	Actual dishwater is a grayish/greyish brown, but combine it with "blonde" and it basically means really light brown but still wanting to call yourself a blonde.
EBONY	Goes together in perfect harmony with ivory; typically synonymous with black or used in place of "nude" by nylon and make-up companies to refer to darker skin tones.
EGGSHELL	The almost white paint color on every new home built like ever; to males – white.
EMERALD	Deep, rich, jewel green often associated with "wicked witches".
FAIR	Usually refers to the pale peach/pink/ivory tones of a Caucasian's skin.
FOREST GREEN	The kind of green you see, in the forest, specifically in the shadows where the sun doesn't reach.
FUCHSIA	Basically magenta, but a lot harder to spell.
GAMBOGE	Mustard yellow, with a slightly prettier name . . . I said *slightly*.
GOLD	Color found at #FFD700; Michael Phelps has like a gazillion medals of this color; whatever you think of him, that guy can swim!
GOLDENROD	Bright yellow, similar to dandelion, but no association to butter.
GRAY/GREY	What happens when ebony and ivory go together like harmony, at least on paper, walls, or canvases as it were.

STILL USEFUL COLOR WORD	STILL USEFUL NOTE ABOUT COLOR WORD
GREEN	Yellow and blue make this; so does the sun when it photosynthesizes plant life; generally used to refer to colors visible between 495-570 nm.
HUNTER	Dark green; hunters really shouldn't actually wear this if they want to be seen and, you know, not shot.
INDIGO	The "I" in "ROYG. BIV"; a deep violet-blue.
IVORY	goes together in perfect harmony with ebony; off-white color similar to stained teeth or elephant tusks
JADE	A color that varies from blue-green to yellow-green, just like the stone it's named for.
JASPER	Gray/grey-green-black - would be an awesome color for eyeliner.
LAVENDER	Light purple like the flower.
LILAC	Light purple, but the flower can actually be light purple, dark purple, pink, or white.
LIME	Bright, almost *neon* green.
MAGENTA	Basically fuchsia, but a lot easier to spell.
MANILLA	Brownish cream, like the envelope or file folder.
MAROON	Reddish brown, unlike a macaroon which is a delicious coconut cookie; if you're macaroon is maroon, it's burnt.
MERLOT	Light but deep reddish purple, just like the wine.
MIDNIGHT BLUE	Basically black - you'd have to have perfect vision to tell the difference, unless you're wearing midnight blue socks with black slacks - then, it's obvious and the whole world can tell.
MINT GREEN	Very light green.
MOSS	Somewhere between grass green and lime green.
NAVY BLUE	Deep blue, like the uniforms in the navy or Catholic school.
NICKEL	Silver and white . . . Together
NUDE	Between lightest brown and cream; a generalized "nude" color.
OATMEAL	Good to eat, not to use as a color . . . Grayish/greyish, beigish.
OLIVE	Green . . . Like a green olive . . . And usually drab. (!)
OPAL	Iridescent, reflective white; opals (the stone) can actually be any color from white to black and even speckled with colors ranging from ROY-G to BI (opals don't usually have much violet…)
ORANGE	Red and yellow make this and so do orange trees, when they grow their fruit; a range of colors visible at 590-620 nm.

STILL USEFUL COLOR WORD	STILL USEFUL NOTE ABOUT COLOR WORD
PEA	Exorcist green. (Think about it. Or don't.)
PEA GREEN	Somehow sounds more disgusting than just "pea".
PEACH	Orangish pink; can refer to skin tones, particularly after bad spray tans.
PERIWINKLE	Pastel blueish-violet color located at #CCCCFF, similar to lavender.
PEWTER	Deep blackish silver; can have hints of blue and/or green.
PINK	Red mixed with white; used to refer generally to light shades of red; different shades of pink can be referred to by rose, salmon, baby pink, pastel pink, coral, pale red and blush; the shade of pink can also change its connotation (e.g., baby pink = innocence, childhood, baby; hot pink—particularly combined with navy blue or black—equals punk vibes and seduction); it's a very confusing color masquerading as plain old red and white.
PORCELAIN	Even lighter than fair, this usually refers to a skin tone that is nearly white.
PUCE	A darkish red.
PUMPKIN	While pumpkins are a bright orange, the color "pumpkin" is usually referring to a brownish orange.
PURPLE	Red and blue make this and it's also the color of rain . . . According to the artist formerly known as Prince . . . God rest his soul.
RED	The good wine and also the color of lips in the 1950s and a prominent color in every department store on February 14th.
ROSE	Reddish pink; the color of a rose unless it's a white, yellow, red or some other color of rose other than a pink/red color.
ROYAL BLUE	A jewel-toned deep, rich blue.
RUST	Brownish orange; the color of oxidized iron, iron oxide.
SARCOLINE	Flesh-colored - whose flesh? I'm not sure. Kind of gross.
SCARLET	Red, only dirtier and with a twinge of orange; technically located at #FF2400.
SEA GREEN	Aquamarine, only more green, and way less romantic.
SIENNA	Earthy red-brown, like sunsets and the Southwest States in the summer . . . how about we just pause here for a moment?

STILL USEFUL COLOR WORD	STILL USEFUL NOTE ABOUT COLOR WORD
SILVER	Most U.S. coins . . . A white-like, shiny metal color generally found at #C0C0C0, but rarely able to be duplicated on printers.
SKY BLUE	Usually refers to the lighter shades of a blue sky even though the sky, itself, can host an array of colors.
SLATE	Dark, deep gray/grey that is nearly indistinguishable from black.
SMALT	Blue, like the kind of blue on old, fancy tea and serving dishes. Who knew? Smalto, by the way, is the colored glass of Italian mosaics. Schmaltz is something else entirely.
SMOKE	This can cover anything from a range of gray/grey to black and everything made of fabric in a shared apartment or townhouse complex.
STEEL	Dark, iridescent gray/grey.
TAN	Similar to cream, but a bit more brown; sun kissed skin.
TAUPE	Medium brown gray/grey, with some yellow hints; to a male – gray/grey; categorized as a neutral color.
TOPAZ	A prismatic silver color; a color mimicking Al2SiO4 (F, OH) 2 - usually that means blue but really Al2SiO4 (F, OH) 2 can be red, yellow, grey, orangey, brownish, pale green, gold, pink or variations on those shade.
TURQUOISE	A very light blue-green, like the stone (often used in Native American art and jewelry) for which it's named.
TWILIGHT	NOT the book; read "Harry Potter", instead; this means the blue-black color as the sun is almost set.
VERMILION	Reddish-orange but sounds scarier.
VIOLET	Purple colors visible from 380-450 nm.
WHITE	Actually the absence of color but not clear (if talking about ink), or the presence of every color (if talking about light).
WINTER WHITE	Like white, but a tad less white; a white that doesn't match your other white clothes, but you won't notice until you're at work.
WOOD	A deep, rich brown shade which may change depending on the tree, or the age of the wood.
XANADU	Who knew it was a color?! Apparently it's a grayish/greyish green. That does not sound exotic at all.
YELLOW	Daffodils, and the sun, and butter; the slow down color.
YELLOW-GREEN	Like Kermit the frog and baby food.

Word
Word Play!
Play
Word Play!
Word
Play
Play

Word
WORD PLAY!

WORD PLAY . . . YOUR Color Words and Notes

Time to play! You could come up with your own brand new colors, or try to come up with some of those fifty shades of one of the already given colors. It's up to you. Just have fun with the words and find some cool ways that you can use them in your writing, journaling, speaking, and LIFE!

COLOR WORD	STILL USEFUL COLOR WORD NOTE (TO SELF)

100 Still Useful Earth Words

So, it's possible that you are writing a story taking place in outer space, a fictitious world, the far reaches of your creative brain, or whatnot.

If that's you and it will always be you, you probably don't have much use for all of these Terran words and I won't be offended if you pass on by. BUT . . . for we gravity-bound types, there are a lot of ways to use the Earth in writing.

Earth and topography are the heart of symbolism in writing.

Climb a mountain? Achieve a goal!

Cross the water? Overcome an obstacle!

Survive a mudslide? Come out ahead after an overwhelming period!

Drown in lava? Well, you might just be writing a volcano manuscript, then.

Grounding your writing in *actual* real, relatable, well-defined *ground* will provide a realistic setting. Add the symbolic powers of earth terminology and you can really step up your writing, take it to the next level . . . you know, get off that plateau and reach the summit of your creative writing gift . . . you get the idea!

Let's go for 100 Earth words, shall we?

STILL USEFUL EARTH WORD	STILL USEFUL NOTE ABOUT EARTH WORD
AIR	Invisible gas all around us - on earth, it's comprised mostly of hydrogen, nitrogen, oxygen and carbon dioxide.
ALGAE	Tiny forms of plant life that grow on or near water.
ANTHILL	Small or big sand piles with little escape holes at the top for their six-legged inhabitants . . . *always* annoying.
ARCHIPELAGO	A group or chain of islands, like the Hawaiian Islands (or "The Archipelago of Last Years" where Rudolph searched for Baby New Year!)
BARREN	Empty; deserted; desolate; void of life.
BLOSSOM	The flower or bloom of a plant or tree.
BOULDER	Very large rock; can be supplied by ACME and used by Wile E. Coyote.
BOUNTIFUL	Full of life including plants, animals, and resources; a good harvest.
CACTI	Put plainly, the plural of particularly prickly plants. (Say it six times fast, and . . . GO!)
CANYON	Steep cut in the earth, usually forged by moving water, revealing sedimentary layers.
CLAY	Rust-colored thick, moldable mud that can be used in crafting and construction alike.
CLOUD	Fluffy, misty, or ominous; condensed droplets of water which form around nuclei (usually an acidic pollution) in the atmosphere to a visible state; the freeform shapes (in which you can find many descriptive shapes) float about full of moisture that they're waiting to drop.
CONIFEROUS	Cone-bearing trees; trees with needle-leaves.
CONTINENT	A large land mass separated or mostly separated from other land masses by water.
CORE	The middle of the earth made entirely of molten lava
CREEK	Pronounced "crick" or "crEEk" depending on where you're from, it's slightly smaller than a stream.
CURRENT	Pull of the water in a body of water; direction of water flow.
DARK	Not light.

STILL USEFUL EARTH WORD	STILL USEFUL NOTE ABOUT EARTH WORD
DAY	Not night; the period of time between sunrise and sunset; unit of time during which most people are awake and functional; 6am-8pm.
DECIDUOUS	Plants that lose their leaves in the winter.
DESERT	Hot, dry, expanse of land, often with little to no vegetation or animal life; geographical location which receives a total amount of rainfall of less than a set average. Often misspelled "Dessert" which is a much more pleasant thing!
DIRT	Mud . . . but dry.
DRUMLIN	A small hill (usually one of many in a formation) created by glaciers.
EARTHQUAKE	Shifting of the planet's tectonic plates that causes rumbling, shaking, and damage to the world above.
EAST	The direction of the sunrise.
FALL	In the northern hemisphere, the third season of the year, punctuated by changing colors of foliage and cooling temperatures.
FIELD	If you build it, he will come; large grassy area either naturally occurring or manmade; occasionally visited by dead fathers, doctors, and baseball players.
FLOWER	Plant plus some pretty colors decorating the top.
FOLIAGE	Generic term for all plant life, particularly as it falls to earth.
FRAGRANT	Scents, typically of a pleasant nature.
FRUITFUL	Bearing fruit, bountiful.
FUNGUS	Mushrooms, which you can eat, but also toe infections, which you should not; eukaryotic plants of the kingdom fungi (not plant, not animal, but still alive).
GLACIER	Gigantic, slow moving sheets of ice that helped to shape the northern hemisphere of the planet.
GRASS	Not the stuff you smoke; you shouldn't do that, anyway; the stuff you walk on and it's soft between your toes.
GRASSLAND	A large section of land covered in low-lying crops and grasses.
GRAVITY	The force that drags us down.
HIGHLAND	Literally land that is high up or that is full of many high locations.
HILL	A steep incline on the earth as high as 999.99 feet.

STILL USEFUL EARTH WORD	STILL USEFUL NOTE ABOUT EARTH WORD
HURRICANE	A great drink, but also a not-so-great storm known for fierce winds, heavy rains and, at the center, or the (eye), an eerie emptiness marked with an ominous gamboge color (!)
ICE CAP	The frozen top (and bottom) of the planet; a pole.
INLAND	A land-locked piece of earth.
ISLAND	A small piece of earth fully surrounded by water.
ISTHMUS	A small strip of land, with water on two sides, that connects to large masses of land, much like a bridge; think Panama.
LAKE	A considerably-sized usually freshwater (but not always) body of water with a range of sizes from the 82,000 square kilometer Lake Superior bordering Wisconsin, Minnesota, Canada, and Michigan, to the 25 square meter Lake Aiso in Italy.
LAND-LOCKED	Any location primarily surrounded on all sides by land.
LAVA	Molten earth that flows like a river of fire.
LIGHT	Not dark.
LIGHTNING	Electric flash that occurs in storms and extreme heat as clouds create fiction amongst themselves; flashes of light visible during a storm; the cause of thunder.
LOWLAND	Literally land that is low on the scale of sky to sea-level or that is full of many low locations.
MAN-MADE	Not naturally occurring structure, lake, or land feature; also spelled manmade.
MASS	A large quantity of something, whether land or water, or food, or building, or my body after Thanksgiving dinner.
MESA	A flat table-like rise of land, common to desert regions.
MOON	A stellar body seen mostly in the night sky as any portion of a sphere from a tiny sliver to a full circle, pitted with craters, reflecting the sun, and effecting the currents of the water bodies across the entire planet; or, more generally, any celestial body that orbits a planet.
MORAINE	A series of bowl-like dips in the earth left behind by the retreating of the glaciers.
MOSS	A fuzzy, green plant that grows on trees, rocks, and other surfaces; according to wives' tales, and MacGyver, it only grows on the north side.

STILL USEFUL EARTH WORD	STILL USEFUL NOTE ABOUT EARTH WORD
MOUNTAIN	A very high, usually peaked, mound of earth over 1000 ft into the air.
MUD	Like dirt . . . only wet.
NATURAL	Occurring without man's interference . . . unless it's a bodily function. Then, sometimes, man interferes with things like baked beans or the mass left behind on Thanksgiving.
NIGHT	Not day; the period of time between sunset and sunrise; unit of time when more people are generally asleep than awake.
NORTH	The top of the planet . . . where Santa lives; the direction a working compass points, with true north being the point on the earth at which the magnetic field points directly downward; up on a traditional map.
OCEAN	Large saltwater bodies of water; the boarders between oceans are generally political divisions.
PEAK	The very tip of a mountain; summit.
PEBBLE	A very small rock.
PENINSULA	A piece of land surrounded by water on three sides (Florida).
PLANT	Vicious ransom-makers giving us oxygen in exchange for carbon dioxide . . . oh, okay; we'll pay; multi-cellular vegetation.
PLATEAU	A long flat piece of earth at a raised elevation.
POND	A typically freshwater body of water with few to no currents and ample plant life; small lake.
PRAIRIE	A dry grassland marked by fields; area of land with the primary vegetation being grass, shrubs and flowers.
RAINFOREST	Forest having high rainfall; doesn't need to be tropical; the Smoky Mountains in Tennessee are a temperate rainforest!
RIVER	Flowing fresh water that runs in a single direction with a typically faster pace than the waves and currents of lakes and oceans.
ROCK	Somewhere between a pebble and a boulder . . . probably closer to a pebble - a large pebble.
SAND	The debris of ground down rocks and other clutter from the floors of our bodies of water - when superheated to a melting point, it becomes glass . . . but, first, it blisters your feet while you run to the water at the beach on a sunny day.
SEA	A very large body of saltwater.

STILL USEFUL EARTH WORD	STILL USEFUL NOTE ABOUT EARTH WORD
SEA LEVEL	The "zero" level on Earth from which all altitude measures are made; equidistant between high and low tide
SEASON	Four major changes in the tilt of the earth that give us variety in weather patterns, particularly the further you are from the equator.
SEDIMENT	The junk that settles to the bottom of a body of water; includes sand, dirt, debris, pollution, rocks, pebbles, animal remains – whatever.
SHELLS	Luxury homes for all sorts of sea creatures, bras for Disney's half women/half fish people, and capturers of the sound of the waves.
SHORELINE	Where a water body meets a land mass.
SOUTH	The bottom of the planet . . . where penguins live; the point on the earth where the gravitational field points straight up.
SPACE	The final frontier.
SPRING	The start of a new year of seasons, usually marked (in the northern hemisphere) by rain, new blooms on deciduous plant life, and the start of baseball season.
STAR	Distant planets, meteors, and suns from which we are receiving the light some many light years later even while the source is already probably gone; a celestial burning blob of plasma.
STINKY	The scent of decay . . . in animals, plants, and teenage boys' locker rooms.
STONE	Definitely closer to a pebble than a boulder.
STORM	Generic term for any number of atmospheric disturbances ranging from rain sprinkles to category 5 hurricanes.
STREAM	Larger than a creek, but smaller than a river.
SUB-TROPIC	The latitudinal rings around the earth that are considered to be the fringes of the tropics; the tropics is the region between the Tropic of Cancer and the Tropic of Capricorn - generally the subtropics are the regions pole-ward of those latitudes until about 40 degrees in either direction.
SUMMER	The second season of the year marked, in the northern hemisphere, by sun, heat, and baseball.
SUN	The star closest to our planet and therefore serving as our primary heat and light resource.
TAR	Thick black substance from deep in the earth valuable for many resources, but mostly just sticky and stinky.

STILL USEFUL EARTH WORD	STILL USEFUL NOTE ABOUT EARTH WORD
THUNDER	A loud, booming sound that follows lightning; the sound lightening makes; also what you should "bring" to rap battles.
TORNADO	A destruction-inducing, high-velocity wind funnel resulting from two weather fronts of varying temperatures meeting over land.
TREE	A plant having a larger, generally wood stem with leafing (or needling, in the case of evergreens and other coniferous plants) branches.
TROPICAL	The region between the Tropic of Cancer and the Tropic of Capricorn
TSUNAMI	A catastrophic wave event, often following an earthquake, wherein ocean waves can reach heights of more than 100 feet before surging inland at rapid paces, wiping out much of the life in their way. The largest one in recorded history claimed more than 300,000 lives, not counting those that later passed away as a result of disease, infection, or injury.
TUNDRA	The frozen cold version of a desert; latitudinal region of the earth characterized by lower temperatures and resulting low plant and tree growth due to the short growing season and low temperatures.
VALLEY	The lowland between two highlands.
VOLCANO	Usually associated with a mountain peak, volcanoes are openings to the earth's core from which molten lava can freely flow.
WAVE	A rapid-moving swell, usually referring to water.
WEST	The sun sets here.
WINTER	The final season of the year marked, in the northern hemisphere, by cold weather, hot soup, and football.

Word
Word Play!
Play
Word Play!
Word
Play
Play

Word
Word Play!

WORD PLAY . . . YOUR Earth Words and Notes

Time to play! What Earth words can you think of and notes that tell you about the Earth words, what the Earth can bring to mind for a character, how the Earth words can change a scene, or just a note about why Earth words are still useful in your writing? Also, consider specific landmarks, such as Mount Everest, or the Pacific Ocean, or the Irish Highlands, or the Caribbean . . . *where were we?*

EARTH WORD	STILL USEFUL EARTH WORD NOTE (TO SELF)

Are there use_less_ animals? Don't get me wrong; I'm not a fan of mosquitoes or the box elder beetles that take over yards in autumn, but even they help to feed the birds that bring song and color. Dogs and cats have been shown to help in recovery from mental or emotional hardships. Animal life from land to sea to air is all a part of a beautifully integrated ecosystem.

BUT . . .

Let's talk about the usefulness of animals, _specifically_ in writing.

Snakes in writing indicate inherent evil . . . all the way back to the first Book.

Eagles are strong.

Cheetahs are fast.

Rats are dirty.

Dolphins are friendly.

Dogs are loyal.

Cats are finicky.

Fish are cold.

Ants are hard-working.

Owls are wise.

Whales are majestic.

Jellyfish are alien.

Now I don't exactly have one-on-one relationships with all of these creatures of the Earth, but that doesn't mean that I can't find useful fits for them in writing.

Can you?

Here are 100 opportunities to try.

STILL USEFUL ANIMAL WORD	STILL USEFUL NOTE ABOUT ANIMAL WORD
ALLIGATOR	Basically today's dinosaurs - similar to a crocodile, but with a pointier nose.
AMOEBA	Squishy little microscopic organism; moves by pseudopods.
ANT	Six legs, three body parts, freakishly strong; picnic annoyance.
BEAVER	Paddle for a tail, two crazy front teeth, and whiskers, but otherwise kind of cute; makes dams.
BEE	Honeybees are an ecological necessity in order to sustain life; "bee" can also refer generally to flying, stinging insects having a color scheme similar to honeybees (e.g., yellows, whites and blacks).
BEETLE	Four legs, shell-like body, cute when it's a ladybug – not so much when it's in a scene from "*The Mummy*"; insects in the order of Coleoptera.
BIRD	Feathered, flying creatures that sing; warm blooded animal characterized by feathers, wings, a beak, and laying eggs.
BRONTOSAURUS	"Thunder Lizard;" one of the largest dinosaurs to have roamed the earth with a round body, and very long neck and tail; often confused with Apatosaurus (Littlefoot from the Land Before Time).
CARIBOU	Much like a deer, only a whole lot bigger with a giant set of antlers.
CAT	Four-legged, toddler-like, furry, talkative creatures comprising (roughly) more than half of all videos on the internet today.
CHAMELEON	A lizard . . . that changes colors . . . cool.
CHEETAH	In the cat family, this spotted animal is the fastest land animal on the planet.
CHIMPANZEE	One of two living species of the genus Pan (bonobo being the other); when you think monkeys are cute, you're probably actually thinking of chimpanzees. Chimpanzees are cute; monkeys are evil; see monkeys.
CHIPMUNK	Like a squirrel, only smaller, and striped.
CLAM	Commonly used to refer to a two-shelled bivavles; gelatinous animal that sits on the ocean floor in a shell waiting for food to land in its mouth; for some reason considered a happy animal.

STILL USEFUL ANIMAL WORD	STILL USEFUL NOTE ABOUT ANIMAL WORD
COCKROACH	When we're all gone, it will live on; in Texas, they are the size of golf balls . . . *not* cool.
COW	Large, relatively boring animals . . . even their butts are square, but they're holy in India (in the rest of the world, they're usually dinner).
COYOTE	Carnivorous, dog-like animal that travels in packs and howls.
CRAB	Funny-looking, shelled, water creatures with claws for hands and antennae-like eyes; crustaceans with 8 legs and 1 pair of pinchers.
CRICKET	Never stops chirping; considered a sign of good luck in some cultures . . . my basement is not one of those cultures.
CROCODILE	Yep - dinosaurs; these ones have square, flat mouths, but still long and full of teeth.
DEER	Generally used to refer to four-legged horse-like creatures with antlers; includes a large number of animals from moose (largest type of deer), to elk, to pudu.
DODO BIRD	Probably the most famous of the extinct birds.
DOG	Canine; can be used to refer to all types of canine including wild wolves or just the domestic variety of dog.
DOLPHIN	Marine mammal typically regarded as very smart.
DRAGON	Fictional creature with a large, scaly body, snout that breaths out fire, and wings.
DUCK	General name for water-loving birds having webbed feet, including swans, geese, typical ducks, etc.
DUCK-BILLED PLATYPUS	A zoological oddity, animal having a beaver-like body and duck-like bill/head; the only living mammal that lays eggs; essentially all the stuff that was leftover in the creation basket at the end of Creation.
EEL	Water snake that is technically a fish.
ELEPHANT	Large mammals with trunks and large flapping ears native to Africa, India, and Asia.
ELK	Type of deer; large but not as large as moose.
FERRET	Weasel-like animal with a face like Frank Burns. (If you know, you know.)
FISH	An animal that lives in the water, breathes through gills, and has fins (instead of fingers).
FLY	Annoying, doodoo-eating insects . . . not Dodo; it's not their fault.

STILL USEFUL ANIMAL WORD	STILL USEFUL NOTE ABOUT ANIMAL WORD
FLYING SQUIRREL	Type of rodent similar to traditional squirrels but having skin extensions between the fore and hind limbs that, when the limbs are extended, enables the flying squirrel to glide mid-jump, giving an appearance of flying.
FOX	Related to dogs; smallish wild dog usually having a bushy tail and pointed ears . . . pretty, but possibly dangerous.
GERBIL	Type of small rodent often kept as a pet.
GIRAFFE	The largest creature (in height) which walks upright on four legs; the spotted animal with a super long neck; the gestation period for giraffes is 13-15 months.
GOAT	A four-legged creature often raised on farms; *"A box can weigh, feel and sound like a goat, but if it doesn't smell like a goat, it's probably coconuts."* ~Chitters, Curious George, The Monkey Mystery Gift.
GORILLA	Highly intelligent ape having many seemingly human-like qualities; researched extensively by Dian Fossey who is often confused with Jane Goodall (who studied chimpanzees).
GUINEA PIG	Not actually a type of pig, but rather a rodent; called "little sea pig" (Meerschweinchen) in German.
HAMSTER	Easily bred rodent kept as pets or used in lab research.
HAWK	Type of predatory bird, usually smaller than an eagle.
HEN	Female bird, usually a female chicken or fowl.
HIPPOPOTAMUS	One of two types of living species of the family Hippopotamidae - the other is the pygmy hippopotamus; third largest land mammal; "river horse"; contrary to popular belief, not a very good Christmas present unless you're a zookeeper.
HORNET	Not a bee. General term frequently used to refer to mean or angry looking stinging insects. Used interchangeably (albeit incorrectly) with wasp.
HORSE	The 4-legged animal that cowboys ride.
HYENA	Laughing jackal; have a cat-like appearance but actually related to dogs; like Banzai, Ed and Shenzi from *The Lion King*.
IGUANA	The big lizard that *doesn't* change colors.
JAGUAR	A big cat - the only type of panther native to the Americas; somewhere between a leopard and tiger.

STILL USEFUL ANIMAL WORD	STILL USEFUL NOTE ABOUT ANIMAL WORD
JELLYFISH	Gelatinous, stinging sea creature that you can barely see while swimming; super ancient ocean carnivores.
KANGAROO	Large marsupial native to Australia; carries its children (Joeys) in their pouch; like Kanga from *Winnie the Pooh*!
KOALA	A smaller marsupial native to Australia famous for eating eucalyptus and it's "barking" from the Outback's trees.
KOMODO DRAGON	Giant hunting lizard found in Indonesia.
LADYBUG	Small red beetle with black spots; also called ladybirds or lady beetles; considered a sign of luck in many cultures; popular topic of nursery rhymes.
LEOPARD	Slightly smaller than a jaguar and with smaller dots than a jaguar.
LION	Large hunting cat native to Africa; related to panthers, jaguars and leopards; nicknamed "king of the jungle" although their primary habitat is usually savannah and grasslands (some very dry deciduous forest locations too, but not jungle) and also, the Queen runs the family!
LIZARD	General term used to refer to reptiles having four legs, a longer body and a tail - includes iguanas, chameleons and geckos . . . not Geico.
LOBSTER	Steak of the ocean; crustacean with 5 pairs of legs (3 pairs having claws, but most only notice the two front most largest claws/pincers).
MONKEY	General term used to refer to smaller primates which swing in trees and usually have tails that assist in swinging in trees, but not all monkeys have prehensile tails; fear strangers and act out through everything from throwing feces to group maulings.
MOOSE	Largest one of the deer family; can also be used to refer to elk, although moose are bigger.
MOSQUITO	Most annoying insect ever; used in *Jurassic Park* (book and film) as the source of dinosaur DNA.
MOUSE	General term used to refer to tiny rodents having larger ears and a long stringy tail; differentiated from "rats" by size and body shape - mice generally have smaller, rounder bodies than rats.
NIGHT CRAWLER	General term used to refer to really long worms (earthworms); also a specific type of worm in Africa.
ORANGUTAN	Type of ape usually having reddish orange hair.

STILL USEFUL ANIMAL WORD	STILL USEFUL NOTE ABOUT ANIMAL WORD
OWL	Nocturnal bird that hoots; the animal who figured out how many licks it takes to get to the center of a tootsie pop; owls are stereotypically thought of as being smart.
OYSTER	General name used to refer to some bivalves and clams; where pearls come from; actual oysters are usually the ones you eat (Oysters Rockefeller).
PANDA	Black & white bear native to China; eats primarily bamboo; eats, shoots, and leaves . . . thank you, Lynn Truss.
PARROT	Colorful tropical bird, often a pet to pirates; can mimic noises (in English "to parrot" means to repeat).
PEACOCK	A male peafowl; the bird with the large, colorful train or fan of feathers used as a display to court peahens; the term "pea cocking" refers to showing off.
PENGUIN	Flightless bird of the arctic (Antarctic, actually); good swimmers; look like they're wearing tuxedos - some have bowties; Disney made them sing; Dreamworks made them into spies; Mr. Popper made them into mystery solvers; and Morgan Freeman told their story.
PIG	Commonly used to refer to the domesticated, usually pink, four-legged animals having snouts and curly tails; however, "pig" encompasses a larger group of pigs and boars, including wild boars which look an awful lot like R.O.U.S.es.
PIRANHA	South African fish with sharp teeth; native to the Amazon River and other South African bodies of water; usually thought of as aggressive, but research has shown attacks on humans tend to only occur during the dry seasons; mind you, it doesn't feel dry to those who are actually *in* the water.
POLAR BEAR	White bear of the arctic and Antarctic; bear with white fur and . . . get this . . . black skin; considered a threatened species.
PORCUPINE	The rodent-like mammal with the quills; "new world porcupines" are what are found in North and South America, while "old world porcupines" are what are found everywhere else.
PTERODACTYL	First animal identified as a flying dinosaur; proper name "pterodactylus".
RACCOON	"Masked" rodent-like animal; eats anything; native to North America; has dark band of hair near eyes and rings around tail.

STILL USEFUL ANIMAL WORD	STILL USEFUL NOTE ABOUT ANIMAL WORD
RAT	Term generally used to refer to rodents that are bigger than a mouse, usually with smaller ears; frequently used as lab animals.
REINDEER	Pull Santa's sleigh; sometimes called caribou; type of deer; generally live in colder regions.
RHINOCEROS	Large mammal with a nose horn; hunted for the horns which are sold on the black market; the rest of the animal is not used to feed the many people in that region who could use the food.
ROOSTER	Male chicken, it usually makes a crowing sound.
SALAMANDER	Amphibian that looks like a lizard; it can regrow some body parts if lost (like a tail); some can be poisonous - some cultures make a hallucinogenic drink make by soaking such poisonous salamanders in water or another liquid.
SHARK	Fish with a skeleton made of cartilage; not the largest, but probably the most feared creature of the saltwater.
SHEEP	Used to refer to the wooly farm animal in the singular or plural.
SHRIMP	Crustacean that can, despite its name, be rather large!
SNAKE	Legless reptile; If red is with black and yellow – stay away from that fellow!
SPIDER	Arachnid; beneficial for the environment - eats other insects; old wives tale says to always let one spider live to eat the insects that make their way into your house, but then to always let one centipede go a year to eat the excess spiders; common root of fear (arachnophobia); species can be poisonous or not; not insects (no antennae); 8 legs; sometimes many eyes and hair.
STINGRAY	Related to sharks; contain at least one barbed stinger at the tail; tragically killed the Crocodile Hunter, Steve Irwin.
SWAN	Type of water-loving bird known for "mating for life"; usually used to symbolize love, fidelity and beauty; subject in the popular children's tale *The Ugly Duckling*.
TIGER	Largest of the cats; striped as opposed to spotted.
TOUCAN	Like a parrot but with slightly less colorful feathers and a larger, more colorful bill.
TYRANNOSAURUS REX	Characterized in pop culture as the most fierce of the dinosaurs; also the butt of many dinosaur jokes for having small arms.

STILL USEFUL ANIMAL WORD	STILL USEFUL NOTE ABOUT ANIMAL WORD
UNICORN	Mythical horse-like creature having a single horn on its head; usually associated with beauty and immortality.
WASP	Stinging insect similar to bees and hornets; generally identified by the paper-like nest/hive.
WATER MOCCASIN	Type of viper/snake; incredibly venomous with a bite being potentially fatal to even healthy adult humans.
WHALE	Generally used to refer to large marine mammals (but excluding dolphins and porpoises).
WOLF	Wild dog, like Jack London's *White Fang*.
WOOLLY MAMMOTH	One of the last species of mammoth; similar to an elephant but covered with a shaggy coarse coat of hair.
WORM	General term referring to long, slimy invertebrate with no legs; earthworm.
ZEBRA	Black and white striped horse; some can look sort of donkey-like.

Word
Word Play!

Play

Word Play!

Word

Play

Play

Word
Word Play!

WORD PLAY . . . YOUR Animal Words and Notes

Time to play! What Animal words can you think of and notes that tell you about the Animal words? Whether looking to compare your characters to certain creatures, create symbolism, or simply have your character interact with animals as part of his or her characterization or development of the setting, these still useful creatures can help to create more than just our awesomely balanced ecosystem!

ANIMAL WORD	STILL USEFUL ANIMAL WORD NOTE (TO SELF)

85

100 Still Useful City Words

I love being outside as much as the next person, but not every moment is spent away from civilization . . . society . . . metropolitan areas . . . urban centers.

Not every moment is spent away from the city.

This list of words is meant to help you across the genres of writing, across the formats, across the styles and venues.

I'd be remiss . . . negligent to leave out terms for the city and its architecture. Pieces of urban landscapes can represent their equivalents in nature, but typically at a quicker pace, higher adrenaline impact, stronger punch, etc.

You want edge? Swap the branches of a tree for the mirrored windows of a skyscraper.

You want speed? Trade the adrenaline rush of a mountain bike race for the floor of the New York Stock Exchange.

You want beauty? Try a breathtaking performance in lieu of a breathtaking view.

City transportation can be as frightening as a rushing river.

Dark alleys can awaken the same fears as isolated forests at night.

By the way, some of these activities are just a few of the things in the list of 500+ Happenings to Prove Existence. What you feel as a result of them is surely a sentiment found in my book of 700+ Verbal Emojis!

For now, here are your 100 city terms!

STILL USEFUL CITY WORD	STILL USEFUL NOTE ABOUT CITY WORD
ACQUIDUCT	Manmade channel for directing water; originated in ancient cultures
AIRPLANE	Aircraft.
ALLEY	Passage between or behind buildings.
ARCADE	The series of arches - not the gaming store.
ARCHWAY	Passage formed by a curved structure.
ART DECO	Artistic style of the 1920s and 1930s characterized by clean, straight lines and rectangular shapes with geometric accents.
ART DISTRICT	Area of a city known for its theater, performing arts, museums or other entertainment offerings.
AVENUE	Type of street, generally used to refer to a suburban street lined with trees, fences and/or shrubs.
BLACKTOP	Area paved with asphalt.
BOULEVARD	Type of street, generally used to refer to a wide road running through a city or higher traffic area; usually boulevards have a median running in the middle which separates the two directions of traffic, sometimes the median is grassy and the term boulevard can be used to refer to the grassy median..."dancin', shaggin' on the boulevard."
BREEZEWAY	Passage between two structures usually outdoors but covered.
BRIDGE	Road connecting two points generally separated by an obstacle (water, valley, road, etc.).
BUS	Type of public transportation that is a road vehicle carrying many people; can also refer to student movers.
BUS STOP	Designated place for bus to pick up and drop off passengers.
BUSINESS	An establishment offering goods or services.
BUSINESS DISTRICT	Primarily non-residential area of a city.
BUSYNESS	Word generally describing the noise, crowd, hustle and bustle of a major city or other defined location (e.g., time square).
BYPASS	Section of freeway, highway, expressway, or tollway which goes around a city without entering it, usually to avoid traffic and congestion.
CAPITOL	Political center of a city, state, country or other region.

STILL USEFUL CITY WORD	STILL USEFUL NOTE ABOUT CITY WORD
CAR	Personal road vehicle designed to transport 1-6 people . . . more if you're in college and you use the trunk; don't do this.
CHURCH	Building used for religious services, usually Christian.
CITY	Largely and density populated residential area inclusive of a business and/or commercial district.
CONCRETE	Material of sand, gravel or other rock/stone mixed with water and other additives generally having a pourable consistency.
CONSTRUCTION	Annoying, but necessary, state of streets being rebuilt.
COUNTY	A residential area that is not so densely populated and characterized by large plots of land.
COURTYARD	Grassy or garden-containing outdoor area completely surrounded by buildings or found in the center of a building or unit of buildings. Central Park in New York is essentially one, big city-wide courtyard.
CROSSWALK	Designated area for pedestrians to cross a street.
CROWD	Large number of people.
CUPOLA	Small, dome-like structure on the top of a building or tower.
CURB	Edge or fringe of a street, road, or sidewalk.
DETOUR	Rerouted path to a destination, usually due to road closures or construction; also a common source of incredible frustration and unexpectedly running late.
DOME	Can refer to a sports arena or a large hemispherical rooftop.
DOWNTOWN	Acity's geographical core, commercial area, or business zone.
DRIVE	Synonymous with road; or the act of piloting a vehicle.
DRIVE-THROUGH	Establishment offering goods or services to customers without requiring that they leave their vehicle.
DRIVWAY	Usually private portion of road neighboring a property and used by residents or visitors to the property to access the property; a place to park your cars at your home.
EAVES	Where the roof overhangs a building.
ELEVATOR	Lift; people hoist; car in a shaft that moves people up and down using a pulley system.
EL	Form of mass transportation that's like a subway but above ground and usually on raised tracks; Chicago's over/underground train system is called "The El".

STILL USEFUL CITY WORD	STILL USEFUL NOTE ABOUT CITY WORD
EXPRESSWAY	Multi-lane tollway or highway generally providing a more direct path between some of the most popular exit locations of a city's center and major surrounding neighborhoods.
FAÇADE	Exterior or front (face) of a building, although more commonly used to refer to the "fake" or decorative aspects of the exterior of a building . . . or person.
FACTORY	Building in which manufacturing and packaging occurs.
FIRE HYDRANT	Structure connected to a water supply that firefighters can connect hoses to in order to battle fires.
FIREFIGHTERS	People trained in firefighting, rescue, and first aid; most rush out . . . they rush in.
FOUNTAIN	Structure that expels water for drinking or for artistic or decorative purposes.
FREEWAY	Multi-lane expressway or highway that one does not have to pay to use.
GARBAGE	Refuse, litter, trash, debris, pollution, and most of reality television.
GARGOYLE	Creepy little dog-like statue often found on the tops of large old buildings; Quasimodo talks to them in some way, shape, or form, in just about every rendition of *The Hunchback of Notre Dame*.
HAZE	Dusty air, usually in the lower atmosphere; dusty quality can be caused by dirt, pollution, ash, smoke, ice, snow, etc.
HISTORIC	Structure, place, region or article that is famous or important or otherwise pertaining to an identifiable and distinct moment in history.
HOMELESS	State of being without a permanent or longer-term residence; while not unique to major cities, urban centers tend to have more gathering centers and available services to meet homeless needs.
KEYSTONE	Central stone of an arch.
LIGHT	Electric source of illumination.
LITTER	Garbage left around and not put in a proper receptacle.
LOBBY	Waiting room; foyer; entry way of a larger building.
MALL	Building or collection of buildings with stores, restaurants, and other retail establishments; outdoor area somewhat protected by trees, fences, shrubs, etc.

STILL USEFUL CITY WORD	STILL USEFUL NOTE ABOUT CITY WORD
MASONRY	Brickwork.
MONUMENT	Structure paying homage to an event, person or location.
MUNICIPALITY	A city or the services that are provided to the public by a city.
NEIGHBORHOOD	Defined residential area, sometimes named.
OFFICE BUILDING	Workplace; building containing a number of businesses.
PARAPET	Protective wall, usually the low wall around rooftops and balconies.
PARK	Public area used for recreation, usually including some green space, a playground or other entertainment for children; a large place for people to gather.
PARKING LOT	Paved surface on which to parka car; "paradise" prior to paving.
PARKING METER	Device at a parking space which collects payment for the time one is parked there.
PARKING STRUCTURE	Multi-level, multi-floor building for storing vehicles when not in use.
PARKING TICKETS	Warnings and fines issued by police or other law enforcement personnel for parking a vehicle in an unpermitted location or for a time longer than what is permitted by law; or, in a city office, your monthly parking fee.
PARKWAY	Street passing through a park, though not really a place to park your car.
PAVERS	Decorative stones and blocks used to make a sidewalk or other outdoor surface.
PILLAR	Support column that is usually decorative or aesthetically pleasing in addition to being a structural support; usually found on old buildings and monuments.
PLAZA	Open public space, usually outdoors; similar to a town square.
POLICE	Law enforcement officers; public servants tasked with enforcing the law and informing the public of the law.
PORTICO	Small section of roof that overhangs a porch and is supported by pillars.
RAMP	Another word for parking structure; also, an on or off path onto a highway.
RED LIGHT DISTRICT	Area known for its….services of ill repute.

STILL USEFUL CITY WORD	STILL USEFUL NOTE ABOUT CITY WORD
ROAD	General term used to refer to a designated path between two locations; paved for the purpose of driving vehicles along it.
ROTUNDA	A building with a generally circular floor plan; or a portion of a building having a generally circular shape with high ceilings.
RURAL	Countryside or relating to the country; a region that is more open land than urban or suburban
SCHOOL ZONE	Area around a school with a lower speed limit.
SIDEWALK	Pedestrian walkway generally on the side of a road.
SKYLINE	Shape of buildings against the sky; silhouette of a city.
SKYSCRAPER	Tall building that seemingly touches the sky.
SKYWALK	Elevated passage between buildings, usually with glass walls.
SMOG	Fog caused by pollution.
SQUARE	Synonymous with plaza, piazza; large public are usually outside and usually at the city center.
STAINED GLASS	Decorative, colorful glass windows usually in churches.
STOP SIGN	Road sign alerting traffic to stop.
STREET	Synonymous with road; a designated path between two locations; usually paved.
SUBURBAN	An area that falls somewhere between rural and urban; usually a residential area just outside of a city proper.
SUBWAY	Underground form of public mass train transportation, but can also refer to an underground pedestrian way.
SURFACE STREETS	Common term to refer to roads which are not part of a highway, freeway, expressway or tollway system.
TAXI	Cars you pay to take you somewhere; aka "Uber".
TOLLWAY	Freeway, expressway or highway for which one must pay a fee to use.
TOWN	Residential area between a city and a village.
TOWN HALL	Civic center of a city or town, or the actual building in which civic leaders meet.
TRAFFIC	Vehicle congestion.

STILL USEFUL CITY WORD	STILL USEFUL NOTE ABOUT CITY WORD
TUNNEL	Underground or covered passage.
UPTOWN	Residential area of a city; sometimes refers to a "higher class" residential area of a city.
URBAN	Relating to the city, as opposed to suburban or rural.
VILLAGE	Defined residential area generally in a valley or other lower region; rural residential area; smaller than a city, smaller than a town, but with residents closer together than a rural area.

Word
Word Play!
Play
Word Play!
Word
Play
Play

Word
WORD PLAY!

WORD PLAY . . . YOUR City Words and Notes

Time to play! What City words can you think of and notes that tell you about the City words? Many of the previous lists were related to naturally occurring things; the list of urban and architectural terms surely opened up a whole new inspiration path for you to build your own list. What are some of the ideas that came to mind and how can you use them in your writing?

CITY WORD	STILL USEFUL CITY WORD NOTE (TO SELF)

100 Still Useful Clothing Words

Coonskin cap or skintight raccoon striped dress? Two very different pictures! Pink polka-dot fluffy robe on a three-year-old in public? Adorable! Pink polka-dot fluffy robe on a thirty-three year old in public? Do you even care? Jeans at a wedding or cocktail dresses? Pulling on the heavy sweatshirt, the fur-lined parka, the windbreaker, or still sweating in your tank top? Chunky pearls (real!) or chunky, colorful bling?

We all judge books by their covers . . . wolves by their skin . . . people by their clothes. Lighten up. I didn't say you were judgmental! But, a judgMENT is made when we see a person's clothing . . . attire . . . dressing . . . wardrobe. We make observations about:

Season
Income Levels
Age
Personality
Priorities
Values

Yeah. Probably a bunch of other stuff, too. If we're making those judgments . . . observations . . . assumptions based on the clothing we see, it's a pretty good guess that we'd be just as likely to draw conclusions when we read about the clothing on characters.

In our journals, we may remember, based on chosen clothing, what we might have felt in specific moments, too. Was it a favorite sweater? Was it the pair of jeans you finally fit back into? Was it the shirt he left behind that still smells like him, or the shirt you wish he would just throw out already?

With hundreds of ideas coming from the clothing described in our writing, here are at least a hundred ideas of clothing words to use!

STILL USEFUL CLOTHING WORD	STILL USEFUL NOTE ABOUT CLOTHING WORD
ANKLET	Bracelet . . . for your ankle.
APRON	Protective garment for while cooking.
BANDEAU	Either a band of fabric used as a headband or a strapless (usually wireless) fabric band used as a bra. Yes; that's right; both a headband and a bra.
BASEBALL CAP	A hat with a bill.
BELT	Something that holds your pants up by going around your waist. Adding holes on the outside feels awful. Adding holes on the inside is a celebration!
BIKE SHORTS	Spandex shorts worn by bike riders . . . and shouldn't be worn anywhere else. No. Really. Please stop.
BIKINI	Tiny swimsuit in two pieces.
BLOOMERS	Puffy pant-like undergarments of the "old days".
BLOUSE	Button-up (or button-down) shirt.
BONNET	Lady's hat made of a usually flimsy cloth with a tie under the chin. Far more common today for babies and young girls.
BOOTS	Protective footwear that usually go up the calf as well; granted, the best boots have nothing whatsoever to do with protection and everything to do with style.
BRA	Support . . . for the ladies.
BRACELET	Anklet . . . for the wrist.
BRALETTE	Usually a wireless, pad-free, and basically useless bra.
BROACH	Large, jewel-containing pin.
CAMISOLE	Lacy tank top undergarment.
CANE	One-stick support that can also look pretty cool with formal attire.
CAP	Head covering.
CAPRIS	Pants that only go down to the knee or calf.
CARDIGAN	An old lady or Mr. Rogers' name for sweater.
CLAM DIGGERS	Capri pants.
CONTACTS	Lenses that stick right to your eye.
CORSET	Thankfully no longer required undergarment that laces and cinches in a waist to the point of restricting breathing.
COVERALLS	Overalls that cover basically everything; or, essentially, the opposite of a bikini.

STILL USEFUL CLOTHING WORD	STILL USEFUL NOTE ABOUT CLOTHING WORD
CUMMERBUND	The colorful thing that goes around the waist as part of a suit; popularized in proms from 1950 to 1999, although they did finally remove the ruffles!
CUP	Protective guard for a gentleman's . . . *parts*.
DAISY DUKES	Shorts that are shorter than short made popular by *The Dukes of Hazard* hottie, Daisy Duke, cousin to Bo and Luke.
DEMI	A bra covering half (or at least not all) of the bust on a woman.
DRESS SHOES	Uncomfortable shoes worn to events, but not always home from those same events.
EARRINGS	Rings . . . for ears.
FLIP FLOPS	Thongs; type of sandals with a strap between the big toe and pointer toe.
FURS	Coats or stoles usually made of real, actual dead animal fur.
FUZZY SLIPPERS	Indoor, usually thin-soled sock-like foot coverings with a cozy, shaggy and/or snuggly inner lining; best when shaped as bunnies.
GARTER BELT	A band usually having some elastic quality which goes around the thighs or waist and has clips to hold up thigh-high or above-knee stockings.
GLOVES	Hand coverings.
GOLLASHES	Willies; rubber boots; splashers, rubbers, puddle jumpers.
GOWN	Floor-length formal dress, usually with a fuller skirt; attire for the formal ball with the prince.
HALTER TOP	A sleeveless shirt which ties around the neck.
HEELS	High-heels; pumps; shoes having a spike for a heel.
JACKET	Outer garment; outerwear.
JEANS	Pants made of denim.
JOCKSTRAP	Support . . . for the gentlemen.
KNEE-HIGHS	Socks or stockings that go up to the knee; also used to refer to boots of the same length.
LEGGINGS	Skin-tight clothing item originally designed to go under dresses, skirts, or long shirts (like tights), but now somehow acceptable as pants, regardless of the level of sheerness!
MAXI	A floor-length dress other than a gown or floor length skirt.
MIDI	Skirt or dress that falls or somewhere between knee and ankle.

STILL USEFUL CLOTHING WORD	STILL USEFUL NOTE ABOUT CLOTHING WORD
MINISKIRT	Skirt that falls above the knee and usually mid-thigh; cause of many a wardrobe malfunction; don't pick that pen up off the floor. Leave it.
MITTENS	Gloves with merged fingers. Actually warmer, but far less efficient than gloves.
NECKLACE	Chain, pendant, lace of sorts, or—occasionally—dog collar worn around the neck.
NEGLIGEE	Unmentionables; teddy; babydoll; usually a sheer/lacy/silky very sexy and short nightgown with matching panties.
NOSE RING	An earring . . . for the nose.
NYLONS	Usually skin-toned, sheer leg coverings, but some can be tinted.
PAJAMAS	Clothes specifically designed to wear while sleeping . . . or studying in college . . . or opening presents on Christmas morning . . . or watching football on New Year's Day . . . or reading a book on a rainy spring morning or brisk start of Autumn!
PANTIES	Female underwear.
PANTS	Slacks; trousers.
PARKA	Very warm, usually puffy, jacket with a hood with a fur trim.
PUMPS	Traditional heels; more modest than a stiletto.
RAIN PONCHO	A plastic or rubber-like shawl to repel water.
RING	A band worn around a finger.
RUBBERS	Rubber protective sleeves for dress shoes so they can be worn in the rain/snow. Typically only for male shoes.
SCARF	Fabric, knit, or crocheted material worn around the neck for warmth or fashion.
SHAPEWEAR	Incredibly tight undergarments worn by females to firm and structure the body (i.e., relocate fat from undesirable positions to create a more desirable shape)
SHAWL	Like a cape, but shorter and usually knit or crocheted.
SHIRT	Clothing of the upper body.
SHORTS	Pants that go down to the knees or shorter.
SKIRT	Pants with no legs.
SKORT	A skirt with shorts built-in underneath for modesty.
SLACKS	Pants; trousers.

STILL USEFUL CLOTHING WORD	STILL USEFUL NOTE ABOUT CLOTHING WORD
SOCKS	Feet coverings that go inside shoes; great for skiing across wooden floors.
SPORT COAT	A dress-attire or business coat that does not exactly match the material of the suit or outfit, but accents it.
SPORTS BRA	Compression undergarment worn by females during exercise or other activity to prevent or reduce bouncing; creator of the "uniboob".
STOCKINGS	Thicker than nylons, thicker than tights.
STOLE	Shrug; a long shawl worn over the shoulders.
STREET CLOTHES	As distinguished from business clothes, gym clothes, or date clothes; in the military and civil services, "civvies."
SUSPENDERS	Garter belt for pants; what your grandfather wears instead of a belt.
SWEATER	Bulky warm shirt, with or without buttons, typically knit or crocheted.
SWEATS	Gym clothes, sweatpants and sweatshirt or t-shirt.
SWEATSHIRT	Like a sweater, but usually pulled over the head; a usually long-sleeved shirt made of a thicker, warmer material and usually considered "active wear"; more likely to have a zipper than buttons.
SWIMSUIT	Bathing suit; bathing outfit; clothing designed to be worn at a beach, pool, or while otherwise engaging in swimming or sunning.
TANK TOP	A sleeveless shirt.
TENNIS SHOES	Generic term encompassing "athletic shoes" or "shoes capable of being worn while participating in an active activity" (e.g., running shoes, jogging shoes, walking shoes, actual tennis shoes, cross-trainers, sneakers, etc.).
THEATER GLOVES	Dressy female gloves that usually go to the mid-arm or elbow and which come in a variety of colors, styles, and fabrics.
THONGS	Can be used to refer to both the undergarment and a pair of flip-flops. So when your dad asks you to grab his thongs, go for the shoes.
TIE	Bow or traditional varieties; fabric worn around the neck usually as part of a suit or tux . . . ***Bowties are cool.**"* ~*The Doctor*

STILL USEFUL CLOTHING WORD	STILL USEFUL NOTE ABOUT CLOTHING WORD
TIGHTS	Thicker than nylons, thinner than tights.
TOE RING	Ring . . . for a toe. Do people still wear these? *Hello 1994 . . . where have you been the last twenty odd years?"*
TOP HAT	Abe Lincoln's hat . . . and Fred Astaire's, too.
TROUSER SOCKS	Socks that are usually just below knee length so that the ends of the socks (or the start of one's leg!) is not showing when you sit in trousers.
TROUSERS	Fancy pants . . . different from the term, "Fancy Pants!"
T-SHIRT	Short-sleeved shirt usually pulled over the head.
TUNIC	Loose garment that's a sort of cross between a dress and a shirt; can be a traditional style garment worn in some cultures.
TUXEDO	Very formal suit; can come with "tails"; traditionally in black and white.
UNDERWEAR	Undergarments; general term for panties and bra for women or boxers, briefs, or . . . other selections . . . for men.
UNMENTIONABLES	Used to refer to any item of clothing which is worn under clothing and not generally seen by the public at large. Not much that's actually un*mentionable* though, these days.
WARM-UPS	Coordinated light wind-breaker style jacket with sweatpants; what athletes wear while preparing (or warming up) for a game; 1980s couples' attire.
WEDGES	Shoes having a wedge-shaped sole, commonly made from cork.
WILLIES	Gollashes; splashers, rubbers . . . you get the idea.
WINTER COAT	Heavy jacket or outer garment suitable for winter-like (cold) temperatures.
WRAP	A style of dress that is wrapped and tied around a wearer; an outer garment that is wrapped around a wearer like a shawl or shrug.
YOGA PANTS	Pants one wears while doing yoga or other exercises. Also worn by busy or lazy females while getting coffee - particularly pumpkin spice lattes.

Word
Word Play!
Play
Word Play!
Word
Play
Play

Word
Word Play!

WORD PLAY . . . YOUR Clothing Words and Notes

Time to play! What wardrobe-centric language can you think of to use in your writing? How do those clothing word-choices affect your characters and scenes? Is the attire helping to bring details to your memory in a journal, or to the life of your character in a story, whether fiction or nonfiction? Now's your chance to expand your still useful clothing word list!

CLOTHING WORD	STILL USEFUL CLOTHING WORD NOTE (TO SELF)

100 Still Useful Home Words

A house is made of brick and stone. A home is made of love, alone.

Home is where you hang your hat.

Home is where the heart is.

You *can't* go home, again.

You can *always* go home.

Home is wherever you're from.

This is my temporary home.

There's no place like home . . . there's no place like home . . . there's no place like home.

Home . . . homemaker . . . homey, which is much different from "*my* homey/homie" and much, much different from homeLY.

Let's keep your writing from being the last of those words with a list of 100 home and household terms that can make your readers feel like they are invited into the most private, precious space that your characters have to offer . . . their homes!

STILL USEFUL HOME WORD	STILL USEFUL NOTE ABOUT HOME WORD
ART	General term referring to decorative knick-knacks or things stuck to a wall (includes paintings, sculptures, and whatever the kids are making in school these days).
BAR	Storage and service area . . . for the booze.
BATHROOM	Full baths have a toilet and a shower or tub while half baths only have a toilet. Technically there's this thing called a ¾ bath, but it's just a full bath with a shower and no bathtub. You learn these things when you buy houses!
BATHTUB	Basin for washing self.
BED	Thing you sleep on, share with pets and children, occasionally watch television from, and . . . other stuff . . . that's not a couch.
BEDDING	The sheets and blankets and pillows and skirts and shams and other decorative and warm-makers that go with or on a bed.
BEDROOM	The room where.....sleeping....happens....
BIKES	Bicycles, tricycles, motorcycles - generally, modes of transportation with less than four wheels
BOARD GAMES	Games to play when bored?
BOOKS	Bound usually white pages covered with usually black or other darker colored symbols which people stare at and vividly hallucinate to forget real life problems and escape to an alternate reality; contrary to public opinion, NOT becoming insignificant in our digital world. Stump done.
BOOKSHELF	Place to store . . . books, of course!
BUREAU	Fancy, and somewhat old-fashioned, word for dresser.
CABINET	General shelving unit, typically hidden by doors.
CARPET	Fuzzy indoor floor covering.
CARS	Autos; vehicles; motorized people transports.
CHAIR	Thing for sitting in; most comfortable in a reclined position.
CHILDREN	Tiny humans, or at least, humans smaller than a full-grown adult.
CHORES	Necessary evils to make sure a household continues to function without major disruption.
CLEANING	Picking up, straightening up, removing clutter/dust/debris, organizing, and doing the dishes and laundry again and again.
CLOSET	Very small room with deceptively large amount of space into which all sorts of objects are shoved to store or hide.

STILL USEFUL HOME WORD	STILL USEFUL NOTE ABOUT HOME WORD
COFFEE POT	Yes, please. Thing that holds the magical brown liquid that helps with, as *The Gilmore Girls* would put it, *" . . . the standing and the walking and the words-putting-into-sentence-doing."*
COOKING	Using heat to transform meat, starches, vegetables and other food products into something edible; or, what the pizza guy does before he shows up at your door.
COUCH	Really long, multi-person, or one-person laying chair.
CUDDLING	Snuggling, relaxing, code for other things.
DECK	Like a patio but usually slightly elevated.
DECORATION	Usually a seasonal knick –knack.
DESK	Flat surface for taking care of business, or stacking up the paperwork of the world.
DINING ROOM	Designated room for eating in that is separate from the room where the cooking happens.
DISHES	Plates, bowls, serving ware; basically anything that food is eaten off of or from.
DISHWASHER	Machine that washes dishes; not your wife.
DOOR	Portal; point of ingress or egress usually selectively blocked by a form of climate control; also on hearts, minds, bodies, souls, and secrets!
DRESSER	Multi-drawer piece of bedroom furniture in which to hold clothes, sometimes with an affixed mirror.
DRIVEWAY	Small private road leading to ones property in order to access the property - usually used to park cars on or play basketball in.
DRYER	Machine that dries clothes; makes them softer than a clothesline outside, but they smell better from the line.
EASY CHAIR	Comfy plush cushioned chair; NOT so *easy* to get out of!
EXERCISE ROOM	Room designated for engaging in physical activity for the purpose of working out; often used for folding laundry or collecting dust!
FAMILY	A group of people with a common bond, whether it be blood, interest, or simply enjoyment (or tolerance) of each others' company.
FATHER	A male head of house, usually the paternal contributor of chromosomes to an offspring.
FAUCET	Tube that water comes out of that's attached to a sink.
FENCE	Outdoor barrier; build more bridges.

STILL USEFUL HOME WORD	STILL USEFUL NOTE ABOUT HOME WORD
FIRE PIT	Hole in ground, sometimes lined with stone, brick, or a metal wash basin, containing fire.
FIREPLACE	Safe location to start an indoor fire.
FLOOR	Thing you walk on inside.
FLOWER BED	Section of earth specifically prepared to grow blooming plants.
FLOWERS	The very blooming plants I speak of . . . BLOOMING not to be mistaken with "Flipping," "Bloody," "Bleeping," plants which are those that don't usually bloom at all.
FOYER	Entryway.
FREEZER	Ice chest; climate controlled cabinet with a temperature below freezing.
GARAGE	House . . . for your cars.
GUESTS	Visitors; people at a location who do not inhabit the location; folks who were in the neighborhood and dropped in—make them some Sanka and pull out the good dessert . . . you know . . . the cookies you did *not* burn!
HALLWAY	Passage from one room in a building to another; often lined with photographic memories.
HEATER	Furnace; also the small space version for reaching those spaces that the furnace does not.
HOME PHONE	A phone number designated to a building rather than a person; quickly becoming obsolete.
KEY	Usually small, metal piece of hardware with a specific pattern of cuts, engravings and ridges used to unlock something without damaging it; giant ones to cities given away to important people . . . those ones don't actually unlock anything.
KITCHEN	Room where cooking and baking happen . . . or are supposed to happen.
KNICK KNACKS	Things that sit on shelves and take up space, usually having sentimental or emotional stories.
LANDSCAPING	Artistic or aesthetically pleasing outdoor formations and organization of plants, trees, shrubs, lawn, stone, sitting areas, animal feeding places, birdbaths, fountains, pools, and—occasionally—plastic wildlife, despite its lack of aesthetic.
LAUNDRY	Dirty clothes . . . or just the dirt on the people who wear them.

STILL USEFUL HOME WORD	STILL USEFUL NOTE ABOUT HOME WORD
LAWN	Yard; grassy part of one's property; greenest on your own side of the fence when you take the time to water it.
LOCK	What a key opens.
LOVE	Affectionate feeling for another; indescribable, immeasurable respect, affection, and desire to be around, help, nurture, and support another person besides yourself; the greatest of faith, hope, and love.
MICROWAVE	Thing that uses radiation to cook . . . yep.
MIRROR	Reflective glass.
MOTHER	A female head of house, usually the maternal contributor of chromosomes to an offspring.
NEIGHBORHOOD	Residential area.
NEIGHBORS	People who live around and next to you.
OFFICE	Room to do work in - like, real work - not "work".
OVEN RANGE	Stovetop; stove with an oven below it.
PAINT	Tinted pasty liquid applied to walls and ceilings.
PATIO	Like a deck, but usually not elevated; outdoor space adjacent a building.
PET FENCE	Barrier to contain a pet . . . can be physical or a buried wire making it appear *invisible.*
PETS	Domesticated animals; some people think they are children.
PHOTO ALBUMS	Bound pages containing photographs or pictures to look back at and enjoy.
PICTURES	Snapshots, photographs, prints.
PILLOW	Cushion to sleep on or put behind your back or in a hug or between your knees.
PLAYROOM	Room to play in; usually a room filled with toys for children to make and keep a mess in.
PORCH	Area directly outside a door.
REFRIGERATOR	Climate controlled cabinet having a temperature of less than room temperature but greater than freezing.
SHELF	Ledge; narrow flat surface to put things on.
SHOWER	A stand-up bath where you don't sit in your own washed off dirt.
SINK	A basin for washing hands, dishes, other smaller objects.

STILL USEFUL HOME WORD	STILL USEFUL NOTE ABOUT HOME WORD
SLEEPING	Wonderful activity that takes place usually at night and usually in a bed; a state of unconsciousness; sometimes a code word for other adult activities that are not even close to sleeping or, if they are, you're doing them wrong.
STOVE	Range; heated surface in a kitchen used to cook.
TABLE	Encompasses any number of flat surfaces in a home.
TABLECLOTH	Fabric that covers a table.
TELEVISION	TV, boob tube, idiot box, one-eyed babysitter (don't – just don't).
THROW RUG	Area rug; moveable rug.
TO-DO LIST	Running, itemized description of things that need ("need") to be done; list of things to nag a husband about; the arbitrary listing of things you hope to get done and then judge yourself a failure by when the number of items crossed out is less than stellar.
TOILET	Porcelain throne; potty seat/chair, commode, head . . . and on and on I could go.
TOOLS	Device used to accomplish a particular task; items used in performing a specific activity ("garden tools").
TOWEL	Medium-sized fabric sheet usually used for drying and usually made of terrycloth.
UTENSILS	Tools for eating with.
WALL	Vertical permanent room divider.
WALLPAPER	Supposedly decorative sticky paper used to cover walls; alternative to paint; most annoying stuff to remove.
WARDROBE	Fancy name for closet; a standing closet (not built in).
WASHCLOTH	Small fabric sheet usually used for washing/wiping and usually made of terrycloth.
WASHER	Machine that washes clothes.
WATER HEATER	Boiler; thing that heats water for showers and washing.
WINDOW	Small portal to the outside world; glass panes in a wall that show the other side of the wall.
WOODWORK	General term for smaller household elements made of wood (e.g., toe boards, baseboards, door frames, etc).
YARD	Lawn, the part of a person's residential property that is not covered by building.

Word

Word Play!

Play

Word Play!

Word

Play

Play

Word

WORD PLAY!

114

WORD PLAY . . . YOUR Home Words and Notes

Time to play! What home words can you think of? Everybody's home is different, so odds are pretty good that you have a completely different subset of terms for your house, the people in it, the things they do, the neighborhood it lies in, and so forth, than another writer. What makes home . . . HOME? What is it for you and how is that important to your writing?

HOME WORD	STILL USEFUL HOME WORD NOTE (TO SELF)

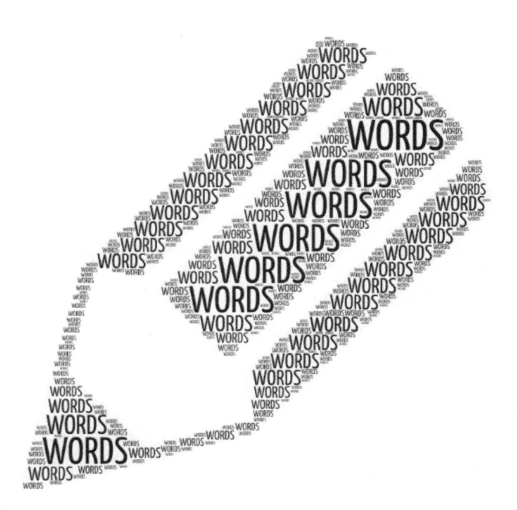

BONUS WORDS . . . YOUR Categories, Words, and Notes

We barely scratched the surface!

According to the Global Language Monitor, the English Language contains 1,025,109.8 words. Kind of makes you wonder what they consider .8 of a word. Like, was someone interrupted mid-word (halfway through a really important discovery) by a heart attack? He never recovered, but the Global Language Monitor just decided that whatever he was addressing was so vital, that they should count the portion of the word that he managed to verbalize before cardiac arrest took over? Or, was it a life word, rather than a life-claiming one? You know the ones. When babies and toddlers speak their first words, they know EXACTLY what they mean . . . even if nobody else does. So, that .8 of a word uttered by the child *must* count for something. Seriously! How does .8 of a word happen?

Soap box . . . away.

As you went through this list of 1000 or so words, with an Easter egg or two mixed in, you surely came up with some ideas of your own about important words, what categories they might fall into and how they could be powerful tools in your writing. We talked about weather, color, animals, and Earth being great symbols. Clothing creates character. Home, food, and beverages make moments and people relatable. City terminology is the faster-paced, adrenalized "landscape" for your writing, and it's our job to see the small, random objects in the midst of greater scenes, happenings, and verbal emojis.

Now, it's your turn to play! ***Make 1000 just the beginning!***

YOUR WORD	YOUR WORD'S CATEGORY	STILL USEFUL WORD NOTE (TO SELF)

Afterword

*You were promised 1000+ words in the title, and I previously mentioned the list would be 1000 words give or take, with mostly give. Those of you paying attention may have noticed that, while words were repeated on some of the lists, there are really, truly, only 987 **different** words described (granted, some of those are on more than one list . . . lobster, for instance, is both an animal and a really yummy food!*

However, those of you paying attention would have also noticed that the main list at the beginning of this book did, in fact, contain 1000 different words. What words those are, well, you should have been paying even more attention. I left you an odd collection of my favorite words.

But that still left the PLUS!

I have this theory that numbers are just evil. They are on nothing good: scales, account balances, age, price, clocks, time, dates, deadlines, speed limits, and "unlucky" number thirteen (the number of favorite words I left you, by the way). So believe me, I was not happy when I counted the words and saw you were owed a PLUS!

This time, however, it seems that the magic of words has overpowered the evil of numbers because I know exactly what to present you with to get to 1001, or . . . officially . . . PLUS.

In this book of useful words, which up until this point included 1000 words, I now hereby officially include.....

REPERTOIRE!

In my repertoire and . . . hopefully . . . in yours.

Fiddlesticks, dumplings and colorblind. How's that for a hammock with a quark?

> *From . . . Sincerely . . . Respectfully . . . Salutations . . . In Closing,*
> *~Laura*

Resources Consulted

Online:
Merriam Webster Dictionary
Oxford English Dictionary
Dictionary.com
Thesaurus.com
Roget's Thesaurus

Experientially:
The Plays We've Experienced
The Books We've Read
The Movies We've Seen
The Songs We've Heard
The Conversations We've OVERheard

Cooperatively:
And Each Other

About the Authors

LAURA GREBE was born . . . arrived . . . was gifted to us on April 24th, 1985, her grandmother's namesake (oh! And Laura Holt from Remington Steele, too). Wife . . . spouse . . . betrothed . . . soul mate . . . other half to Josh Grebe and mother . . . mama . . . female parent . . . mommy . . . to Noah, the big brother Angel looking over his family from heaven, and Maddy, Noah's little sister.

A lifetime Wisconsinite and Patent Law lawyer living in the greater Milwaukee area, Laura knew she wanted to be a lawyer since the first grade when she started reading *Nancy Drew* books. She also loves science; reading (particularly mysteries with Nancy Drew and Sherlock Holmes being the favorites, science fiction, and tweeny-bopper mysteries and science fiction . . . um . . . *in German)*; scuba diving; jumping out of planes (attached to a qualified person wearing a parachute of course); baking cupcakes (aka: playing cupcake wars in her kitchen); showing Maddy the world; church; singing in the car (these days, usually to *Mickey Mouse Club*, *Doc McStuffins*, *Sofia the First*, and *Bubble Guppies*), and spending way too much money on Zulily and Shutterfly.

Laura's *500+ Happenings to Prove Existence*, *700+ Verbal Emojis*, and *1000+ Still Useful Words* were born out of her *Maternity Journal*. (Stay tuned! It's coming; we promise!) Through the unimaginable loss of a son that occurred before her pregnancy with Maddy, she and her husband, Josh, recognized the impossible relatability of journals to a grieving person who fearfully hopes and anticipates new life. Being often laid up during Maddy's prenatal days, Laura found herself digging deeper than ever to place intentional recognition on the things she did, felt, and observed. To Laura, these lists were tools to help her describe her days' experiences, but her publisher realized that, to the writers and the therapeutic writing journalists they routinely work with, Laura's simple tools were anything but. So came the *Experimental Word Play* series that she now brings you.

She promises the venture into list-land won't change the uniqueness of her, punctuated by decided favorites that keep her connecting to the world and its words including: *animal* – bunny; *salty snack* - popcorn or Tostitos; *sweet snack* – cupcakes (we can't wait to bring you her *Cupcake Therapy* book!); *time of day* - morning sunrise; *season* – fall; *holiday* – Halloween; *color* - green (but not lime green, green green or olive green - more like leafy, natural green); *sport* – soccer; *dream vacation* – London; *drink* – iced tea; *clothing style* – classic, hippy, and/or old-school pin-up (you know, the kind that was sexy but didn't really show anything by today's standards); *music* – country; and *lucky number*– 13, which is how many favorites are listed here!

~~~~

Working with Laura to create the *Experimental Word Play* series was **REJI LABERJE**, Owner and Creative Director of Reji Laberje Writing and Publishing. Reji is a Bestselling Author with nineteen years of professional-level experience in the writing industry and her fortieth book hitting the presses in 2016. Laura's creativity was a joy for Reji to embrace. She looks forward to using the 500+, 700+, and 1000+ for the 20,000+ days she would be lucky to have left on God's green Earth. Also in that time, she intends to continue living life outside of Milwaukee where she resides with her husband of twenty years, Joe, and their active family of seven people and four pets.

Made in the USA
Middletown, DE
26 October 2022